AF591183

History of Nations
3

Ibn al-Jawzi (1116 C.E -1200 C.E)

Alreshah.net

Canada

Copyright © 2018-20 by **Alreshah**

All rights reserved. No part of this publication may be reproduced, distributed, or transmitted in any form or by any means, without prior written permission.

Alreshah
www.Alreshah.net

If any error is found, please contact us through our website alreshah.net.

Book Layout © 2017 BookDesignTemplates.com

History of Natioans 3 / Ibn al-Jawzi. -- 1st ed.
ISBN 978-1-989875-13-1

Contents

CHAPTER 1

Introduction

In the name of God, The Entirely Merciful, the Especially Merciful

This is the translation of the first part in a sequence of books written by Imam Abd al-Raḥmān b. ʿAlī b. Muḥammad Abu 'l-Faras͟h b. al-Jawzi, known as Ibn al-Jawzī. He was an Arab Muslim jurisconsult, preacher, orator, heresiographer, traditionist, historian, judge, hagiographer, and philologist who lived in Baghdad during the twelfth century.

In this book, he collected what was known in his time about the nation's history. As the reader will note, this book focused first on parts more toward the Middle East region and on the prophets known to Jews and Christians. The reason behind this is that Baghdad was the heart of the Islamic world, and most of the other nations' knowledge had been concentrated in Baghdad in the Golden Age of the Islamic Empire.

It is essential to understand that the first and second part of this book, until 600 AD, was based on what the Imam read and gathered from Israelites known to him in his time. So, similarities might be found between the historical events mentioned in those two parts and Biblical stories.

Starting from the end of the second book onward, the authentication differs hugely, as those are more related to Islamic history and the states surrounding the Islamic empire. The spread of knowledge and literacy within the Islamic world resulted in better record-keeping, and references to an event were recorded in different documents.

That what makes this book one of the important books in the history of the region, especially from 600 AD to the author's death, which will be in part three onward.

• CHAPTER 2 •

The 9th year of his prophethood (PBUH)

Boycotting of Banu Hashim

Scholars differed regarding the violation of the document:

First: God, Exalted is he, told His Prophet (PBUH) about that the termite ate all oppression and injustice in it. By turn, the Prophet (PBUH) told his uncle Abu Talib about that, he then told his brothers about the same. They decided to go to disbelievers of Quraysh and told them about this accident which the Prophet (PBUH) told them; he told Quraysh "if what the Prophet (PBUH) said was true, you would believe him, if not I would give him to you whether to kill or let him live". They agreed. They went to get the document and when they found that what the Prophet

(PBUH) told them was true, they hung down their heads. Abu Talib said to them that they were wrong and aggressive, they are deserve to be abandoned.

Second: Hisham ibn Amr ibn Alharith Al'amery went to Zuhair ibn Ummayya ibn Almughirah and said "Are you pleased that you can eat food, wear clothes and marry to women while your maternal uncles cannot buy or sell and marry?." He told Hisham: "Woe to you, what can I do? I am just one man. I swear to God if there is just a man with me, I will violate it." Hisham said: "Here I am with you." Zuhair said: "We want a third one". Hisham went to Almut'am ibn 'Umair and said: "Do you agree that two clans of Banu Abd Manaf to be died". He said: "Woe to you! What can I do? I am just one man". Hisham said: "You found a second man." He answered: "We need a third one" Hisham said: "There is Zuhair ibn Banu Ummayya" He said: "We need a fourth one" Hisham went to Abu Albukhturi ibn Hisham and told him the same as he told Almut'am and he agreed to be the fourth man. But he told Hisham that they needed a fifth one. Hisham went to Zum'ah ibn Asad and agreed to be with them. They decided to breach this boycott document. They went to Kaaba and told people that this document was oppressive to Banu Hashim and they did not agree upon its content. One of them went to cut the document but he found that the termite ate it except the phrase of 'In the name of God'.

Ibn 'Abbas reported: Dimad came to Mecca and he belonged to the tribe of Azd Shanu'a, and he used to protect the person who was under the influence of charm. He heard the foolish people of Mecca saying that Muhammad (PBUH) was under the spell. Upon this he said: If I were to come across this man, God might cure him at my hand. He met the Prophet and said: Muhammad, I can protect (one) who is under the influence of charm, and God cures one whom He so desires at my hand. Do you desire (this)? Upon this, the Messenger of God (PBUH) said: Praise is due to God, we praise Him, ask His help; and whom God guides aright, nobody can mislead him, and he whom caused His dissatisfaction, nobody can guide him, and I bear testimony to the fact that there is no deity but God, He is One, having no partner with Him, and that Muhammad is His Servant and Messenger.

Now after this he (Dimad) said: "Repeat these words of yours before me", and the messenger of God (PBUH) repeated these to him thrice; and he said: "I have heard the words of soothsayers, the words of magicians, and the words of poets, but I have never heard such words as yours, and they reach the depth (of the ocean of eloquence) ; bring forth your hand so that I should take oath of fealty to you on Islam." So he took an oath of allegiance to him. The Messenger of God (PBUH) said: "It (this allegiance of yours) is on behalf of your people too." He said: "It is on behalf of my people too." The Messenger of God (PBUH) sent a brigade. The leader said to the brigade when passed by Dimad's people: Did you find anything from these people? One of them said: "I found a utensil for water". Upon this, the commander said: "Return it, it is for Dimad's people".

CHAPTER 3

Tale of events that had occurred during the 10th year of his prophethood (PBUH)

Death of Abu Talib

Abu Talib died in Shawal in this year, he was some of 80 years old.

When Abu Talib was sick, the Prophet (PBUH) entered to him and invited him to Islam.

It is reported by Sa'id ibn Musayyib who narrated it on the authority of his father (Musayyib ibn Hazm) that when Abu Talib was about to die, the Messenger of God (PBUH) came to him and found with him Abu Jahl (Amr ibn Hisham) and 'Abdullah ibn Abu Umayya ibn Almughirah. The Messenger of God (PBUH) said: "My uncle, you just make an utterance that there is no deity but God, and I will bear testimony before God (of your belief)", Abu Jahl and 'Abdulla ibn Abu Umayya addressing him said: "Abu Talib, would you abandon the religion of Abdulmutalib?" The Messenger of God (PBUH) constantly requested him (to accept his offer), and (on the other hand) was repeated the same statement (of Abu Jahl and 'Abdullah ibn Abu Umayya) till Abu Talib gave his final decision and be stuck to the religion of Abdulmutalib and refused to confess that there is no deity but God. Upon this the Messenger of God remarked: By God, I will persistently beg pardon for you till I am forbidden to do so (by God), It was then that God, the Magnificent and the Glorious, revealed this verse: "It is not for the Prophet and those who have believed to ask forgiveness for the polytheists, even if they were relatives, after it has become clear to them that they are companions of Hellfire"." مَا كَانَ لِلنَّبِيِّ وَالَّذِينَ آمَنُوا أَن يَسْتَغْفِرُوا لِلْمُشْرِكِينَ وَلَوْ كَانُوا أُولِي قُرْبَىٰ مِن بَعْدِ مَا تَبَيَّنَ لَهُمْ أَنَّهُمْ أَصْحَابُ الْجَحِيمِ" (9: 113).

It is narrated that Abu Talib said to the Prophet (PBUH) "If it was not my fear that Quraysh would say that I entered to Islam because of fearing death, I would do what makes you please". Abu Talib told Banu Abdulmutalib that they would be fine and in good conditions as long as they listened to and followed him

(PBUH); he advised then to follow and help the Prophet, to be guided.

The Prophet (PBUH) said: "Why do you commend them and do not follow it!?" Abu Talib said that if the Prophet (PBUH) asked him to say it while he was in a good health, he would say it, but he feared that Quraysh say that he said it while he was dying, fearing death and he denied it while he was in a good health.

It was narrated by Ali (May God be pleased with him) when he went to the Prophet (PBUH) and told him that Abu Talib died. The Prophet cried and said: "Go to wash him, put him in a coffin and bury him, may God forgive and be merciful to him."

Ali said: "I did. The Prophet (PBUH) continued to ask forgiveness for him for days till Jibril revealed this verse to him (PBUH): 'It is not for the Prophet and those who have believed to ask forgiveness for the polytheists, even if they were relatives, after it has become clear to them that they are companions of Hellfire"." مَا كَانَ لِلنَّبِيِّ وَالَّذِينَ آمَنُوا أَن يَسْتَغْفِرُوا لِلْمُشْرِكِينَ وَلَوْ كَانُوا أُولِي قُرْبَىٰ مِن بَعْدِ مَا تَبَيَّنَ لَهُمْ أَنَّهُمْ أَصْحَابُ الْجَحِيمِ" (9: 113).'".

Death of Khadija

Khadija (May God be pleased with her) died several days after Abu Talib.

It is narrated that a month and 5 days separated the death of Abu Talib and that of Khadija. They were two disasters that afflicted the Prophet (PBUH) where he stayed at home and went out fewer as Quraysh annoyed him more than ever. Abd Al'uzzā ibn Abd Almuttalib (Abu Lahab) went to the Prophet (PBUH) and said to him that he could get out and do anything as long as he (Abu Lahab) was alive. One of Quraysh disbelievers insulted the Prophet (PBUH), Abu Lahab went to him beating. The man cried and told that Abu Lahab loved the Prophet. Quraysh gathered and asked him if he was still believing in the religion of Abdulmutalib or not. Abu Lahab told them I did not leave my father's religion but I intended to protect my nephew whenever he went and whatever he wanted. The Prophet was going and returning without any intrusion from any Qurayshi till Abu Jahl went to Abu Lahab and told him that his nephew (PBUH) was saying that Abdulmutalib was going to enter the Hell. Abu Lahab went to the Prophet (PBUH) to make sure that if he said that. The Prophet said: 'Yes'. Abu Lahab declared that he became an enemy to the Prophet (PBUH) as long as the Prophet (PBUH) said that Abdulmutalib would enter the Hell. Then, Qurayshi men were very hostile to the Prophet (PBUH). The Prophet (PBUH) and Zaid ibn Haritha went out to Ta'if in the 10th year.

It is said that he stayed at Ta'if for ten days and some said for a month inviting all its honored men to worship God but they feared for their children and asked him to get out from the city, letting their children and silly people to throw him with stones till his leg bled and his head was cut while Zaid was protecting him by himself.

The Prophet left Ta'if returning to mecca while he was very heartbreaking. Zaid said to him (PBUH) 'How do you return after they forced you go out?"

He sent a man from Banu Khuza'a to Mut'am ibn 'Udai asking him to enter Mecca under his protection, he said 'Yes'.

It is said that while the Prophet (PBUH) was in Ta'if, he went to honored men of Banu Thaqif inviting them to Islam but they refused and asked him to go out from their city and let the silly people to throw him (PBUH) with stones.

The Prophet (PBUH) reached a garden for Utbah ibn Rabi'ah and his brother Shaibah who asked a servant, called 'Addas, to give the Prophet (PBUH) a bunch of grape. The Prophet asked 'Addas: "Where are you from?" He answered that he was from people of Nineveh. The Prophet (PBUH) said "Are you belonging to the righteous man Jonah ibn Amittai?" 'Addas said: "How do you know this man?" the Prophet answered: "He is my brother, he was a prophet and I am a prophet". In that time, 'Addas started to kiss the head, hands and legs of the Prophet (PBUH).

His return to Mecca

From events: the Prophet sent for many men asking their protection to enter Mecca but they refused except Almut'am ibn 'Udai who accepted.

The Prophet (PBUH) entered Mecca and stayed there till the season of pilgrimage. He was standing among pilgrims saying: "O clan of so, I am the prophet of God Who asking you to worship no one but Him." meanwhile, Abu Lahab was standing behind him saying to people: "Do not believe him". The Prophet (PBUH) was going to every clan and inviting them to worship God but they all refused and badly responded to him.

Marriage of the Prophet (PBUH) to 'Aisha (May God be pleased with her)

From events of that year: Marriage of the Prophet to 'Aisha and Sawda.

It is narrated that when Khadija died, Khawlah bint Hakim, the wife of Uthman ibn Maz'oon went to the Prophet (PBUH) offering him to marry. The Prophet said: 'Who' She said: 'Virgin or widow?' The Prophet said: "Who is the virgin" she answered that she was the daughter of Abu Bakr.

The Prophet asked her about the widow she told him that she was 'Sawda bint Zam'a' the Prophet asked her to go to them telling them about the Prophet.

Khawlah bint Hakim went to the wife of Abu Bakr and told her about the Prophet's proposal to marry 'Aisha. Abu Bakr said that she was the daughter of his brother. Khawlah bint Hakim went to the Prophet (PBUH) telling him about that. The Prophet (PBUH) told her that Abu Bakr was his brother in Islam and he can marry to his daughter. Khawlah went to Abu Bakr and told him what the Prophet (PBUH) said. Abu Bakr invited the Prophet (PBUH) to go to him and married 'Aisha to him while she was 6 years.

Khawlah went to 'Sawda bint Zam'a telling her about the proposal of the Prophet (PBUH), she agreed.

Khawlah went to her father and told him about the proposal of the Prophet (PBUH), he said that the Prophet (PBUH) was generous and eligible to marry her and he asked about his daughter opinion, his daughter replied: 'Yes'. The father said to Khawlah to invite the Prophet (PBUH) to him and married his daughter to him.

Tale of those who died in this year

- Khadija bint Khuwaylid ibn Asad ibn Abd Al'uzza ibn Qusai ibn Kalib, Umm Hind.

Khadija died in this year while she was 65 years old. She was buried in Jannat Almu'alla cemetery, in Mecca.

- Assakran ibn Amr ibn Abd Shams ibn Abd Wud:

He entered Islam in Mecca and migrated to Abyssinia and his wife 'Sawda bint Zam'a' and he died in Abyssinia and it is said he died in Mecca.

- Abd Manaf 'Abu Talib' (Paternal uncle of the Prophet (PBUH))

CHAPTER 4

Tale of events during the 11th year of his prophethood (PBUH)

Beginning of the entry of Ansar (Helpers) to Islam

The Prophet (PBUH) went out during the season of pilgrimage as he used to do, inviting people to Islam. While he was in Aqaba, he met some people of Banu Khazraj. The Prophet (PBUH) asked them to sit down to invite them to worship God, Exalted is He, invoked them to Islam and recited some Verses of Quran to them. In Medina, Jews were talking about a prophet to be sent during that time so when the Prophet told them that, they believed in him; they were 6 men.

When they returned to Medina, they talked about the Prophet (PBUH) and invited people to Islam and that was all over the city after short time.

CHAPTER 5

Tale of events during the 12th year of his Prophethood (PBUH)

Night Journey and Ascension to the Seven Heavens

It is said that the night journey was at night of 17th of Ramadan in the 12th year of his prophethood (PBUH) before Hijra (Migration to Medina) with 18 months. It is said it was at the night of 17th of Rabi' I before Hijra with a year.

It was at the night of 27th of Rajab

Malik ibn Sa'sa'a said that the Prophet (PBUH) described to them his Night Journey saying, "While I was lying in Al-Hatim or Al-Hijr, suddenly someone came to me and cut my body open from here to here." I asked Al-Jarud who was by my side, "What does he mean?" He said, "It means from his throat to his pelvic area," or said, "From the top of the chest."

The Prophet (PBUH) further said, "He then took out my heart. Then a gold tray of belief was brought to me and my heart was washed and was filled (with Belief) and then returned to its original place. Then a white animal which was smaller than a mule and bigger than a donkey was brought to me." (On this Al-Jarud asked, "Was it the Buraq, O Abu Hamza?" I (i.e. Anas) replied in affirmative. The Prophet (PBUH) said, "The animal's step (was so wide that it) reached the farthest point within the reach of the animal's sight. I was carried on it, and Jibril set out with me till we reached the nearest heaven. When he asked for the gate to be opened, it was asked, 'Who is it?' Jibril answered, 'Jibril.' It was asked, 'Who is accompanying you?' Jibril replied, 'Muhammad.' It was asked, 'Has Muhammad been called?' Jibril replied in affirmative. Then it was said, 'He is welcomed. What an excellent visit his is!' The gate was opened, and when I went over the first heaven, I saw Adam there. Jibril said (to me). 'This is your father, Adam; pay him your greetings.' So I greeted him and he returned the greeting to me and said, 'You are welcomed, O pious son and pious Prophet.' Then Jibril ascended with me till we reached the second heaven. Jibril asked for the gate to be opened. It was asked, 'Who is it?' Jibril answered, 'Jibril.' It was asked, 'Who is accompanying you?' Jibril replied, 'Muhammad.' It was asked, 'Has he been called?' Jibril answered in the affirmative. Then it was said, 'He is welcomed. What an excellent visit his is!' The gate was opened. When I went over the second heaven, there I saw Yahya (i.e. John) and (Jesus) who were cousins of each other. Jibril said (to me), 'These are John and Jesus; pay them your greetings.' So I greeted them and both of them returned my greetings to me and said, 'You are welcomed, O pious brother and pious Prophet.' Then Jibril ascended with me to the third heaven and asked for its gate to be opened. It was asked, 'Who is it?' Jibril replied, 'Jibril.' It was asked, 'Who is accompanying you?' Jibril replied, 'Muhammad.' It was asked, 'Has he been called?' Jibril replied in the affirmative. Then it was said, 'He is welcomed, what an excellent visit his is!' The gate was opened, and when I went over the third heaven there I saw Joseph. Jibril said (to me), 'This is Joseph; pay him your greetings.' So I greeted him and he returned the greeting to me and said, 'You are welcomed, O pious brother and pious Prophet.' Then Jibril ascended with me to the fourth heaven and asked for its gate to be opened. It was asked, 'Who is it?' Jibril replied, 'Jibril' It was asked, 'Who is accompanying you?' Jibril replied, 'Muhammad.' It was asked, 'Has he been called?' Jibril replied in the affirmative. Then it was said, 'He is welcomed, what an excellent visit his is!'

The gate was opened, and when I went over the fourth heaven, there I saw Idris. Jibril said (to me), 'This is Idris; pay him your greetings.' So I greeted him and he returned the greeting to me and said, 'You are welcomed, O pious brother and pious Prophet.'

Then Jibril ascended with me to the fifth heaven and asked for its gate to be opened. It was asked, 'Who is it?' Jibril replied, 'Jibril.' It was asked. 'Who is accompanying you?' Jibril replied, 'Muhammad.' It was asked, 'Has he been called?' Jibril replied in the affirmative. Then it was said He is welcomed, what an excellent visit his is! So when I went over the fifth heaven, there I saw Harun (i.e. Aaron), Jibril said, (to me). This is Aaron; pay him your greetings.' I greeted him and he returned the greeting to me and said, 'You are welcomed, O pious brother and pious Prophet.' Then Jibril ascended with me to the sixth heaven and asked for its gate to be opened. It was asked. 'Who is it?' Jibril replied, 'Jibril.' It was asked, 'Who is accompanying you?' Jibril replied, 'Muhammad.' It was asked, 'Has he been called?' Jibril replied in the affirmative. It was said, 'He is welcomed. What an excellent visit his is!' When I went (over the sixth heaven), there I saw Moses. Jibril said (to me),' This is Moses; pay him your greeting. So I greeted him and he returned the greetings to me and said, 'You are welcomed, O pious brother and pious Prophet.' When I left him (i.e. Moses) he wept. Someone asked him, 'What makes you weep?' Moses said, 'I weep because after me there has been sent (as Prophet) a young man whose followers will enter Paradise in greater numbers than my followers.' Then Jibril ascended with me to the seventh heaven and asked for its gate to be opened. It was asked, 'Who is it?' Jibril replied, 'Jibril.' It was asked,' Who is accompanying you?' Jibril replied, 'Muhammad.' It was asked, 'Has he been called?' Jibril replied in the affirmative. Then it was said, 'He is welcomed. What an excellent visit his is!' So when I went (over the seventh heaven), there I saw Abraham. Jibril said (to me), 'This is your father; pay your greetings to him.' So I greeted him and he returned the greetings to me and said, 'You are welcomed, O pious son and pious Prophet.'

Then I was made to ascend to Sidrat-ul-Muntaha (i.e. the Lote Tree of the utmost boundary) Behold! Its fruits were like the jars of Hajr (i.e. a place near Medina) and its leaves were as big as the ears of elephants. Jibril said, 'This is the Lote Tree of the utmost boundary) . Behold ! There ran four rivers, two are hidden and two are visible, I asked, 'What are these two kinds of rivers, O Jibril?' He replied,' As for the hidden rivers, they are two rivers in Paradise and the visible rivers are the Nile and the Euphrates.' Then Al-Bait-ul-Ma'mur (i.e. the Sacred House) was shown to me and a container full of wine and another full of milk and a third full of honey were brought to me. I took the milk. Jibril remarked, 'This is the Islamic religion which you and your followers are following.' Then the prayers were enjoined on me: They were fifty prayers a day. When I returned, I passed by Moses who asked (me), 'What have you been ordered to do?' I replied, 'I have been ordered to offer fifty prayers a day.' Moses said, 'Your followers cannot bear fifty prayers a day, and by God, I have tested people before you, and I have tried my best with Banu Israel (in vain). Go back to your Lord and ask for reduction to lessen your followers' burden.' So I went back, and God reduced ten prayers for me. Then again I came to Moses, but he repeated the same as he had said before.

Then again I went back to God and He reduced ten more prayers. When I came back to Moses he said the same, I went back to God and He ordered me to perform ten prayers a day. When I came back to Moses, he repeated the same advice, so I went back to God and was ordered to observe five prayers a day. When I came back to Moses, he said, 'What have you been ordered?' I replied, 'I have been ordered to perform five prayers a day.' He said, 'Your followers cannot bear five prayers a day, and no doubt, I have got an experience of the people before you, and I have tried my best with Banu Israel, so go back to your Lord and ask for reduction to lessen your follower's burden.' I said, 'I have requested so much from my Lord that I feel ashamed, but I am satisfied now and surrender to God's Order.' When I left, I heard a voice saying, 'I have passed My Order and have lessened the burden of My Worshipers."

It is narrated that when the Prophet (PBUH) waked up on the morning after Night Journey in Mecca, he was outraged as people would never believe his tale. He sat, immersed in sadness when

Abu Jahl passed by him asking (PBUH) if there was something happened, the Prophet said 'Yes' and told him that he was in a night journey. Abu Jahl said 'Where?' The Prophet (PBUH) answered to Jerusalem, Abu Jahl said to him then you waked up among us? He (PBUH) said 'Yes'. Abu Jahl cried "O people of Banu Ka'b ibn Lu'ayy, come!" People gathered around him and he told the Prophet to tell them the tale.

The Prophet (PBUH) repeated the same talk and he repeated the same dialogue. People asked the Prophet (PBUH) to describe the Masjid. When the Prophet (PBUH) was describing the Masjid, there was a picture for the Masjid was put before him. People said that it was a right description.

Tale of Al Aqaba I

It is one of the most prominent events of that year:

When the Prophet (PBUH) went out to the season of pilgrimage, there were some people of Alansar, twelve men, who met him at Aqaba where the Prophet (PBUH) accepted their pledge of allegiance.

Ubada ibn Assamit said: "We pledged allegiance to the Prophet (PBUH) on day of Aqaba I when we were 12 men. We pledged allegiance to the Prophet (PBUH) that we will not worship nothing but God, will not steal, commit adultery, kill our children, slander, and obey him" The Prophet (PBUH) said "If you were sincere to that, you would enter the Heaven."

The Prophet (PBUH) sent with them Mus'ab ibn 'Umair to acquire them knowledge and recite Quran to them. He was the guest of As'ad ibn Zurarah.

Once, Sa'd ibn Mu'adh went to Usayd ibn Hudayr asking him to go to As'ad ibn Zurarah to stop him as there was a strange man who say nonsense to people.

Usayd ibn Hudayr went to As'ad ibn Zurarah complaining the strange man, Mus'ab ibn 'Umair, they asked him to sit down and listen. Mus'ab ibn 'Umair told him about Islam and recited Quran to him.

When Usayd ibn Hudayr listened to Mus'ab, he accepted Islam and testified that there is no deity but God and Muhammad is His Prophet.

Sa'd ibn Mu'adh went to Mus'ab ibn 'Umair who told him about Islam, then, Sa'd ibn Mu'adh entered into Islam.

Sa'd ibn Mu'adh went to Banu Abdul-Ashhal where they were at their meeting place, he asked them how they knew what had happened to him. They replied "You are our Chief, the most active in our interests, the best in your judgment, and the most fortunate in leadership." He then said: "I will not speak to a man or a woman among you until you believe in God and his Apostle." As a result every man and woman among Banu Abdul-Ashhal joined Islam.

Tale of events that had occurred during the 13th year of his prophethood (PBUH)

Tale of Aqaba I

The Prophet (PBUH) went out during the season of pilgrimage where he met a group of Alansar who pledged allegiance to the Prophet (PBUH).

Ka'b ibn Malik said that he and his people went to Mecca and they met the Prophet (PBUH) and set a date to meet him in Aqaba. "When it was the night we set, we went out to our date with the Prophet (PBUH) till we met together at a mountain (Aqaba). We were seventy-three men and two women. The Prophet came with his uncle 'Abbas ibn Abdulmutalib while he was embracing the religion of his people to be sure about his nephew's safety."

'Abbas talked first and told them "The Prophet is among his clan protected and glorified but he wanted to migrate to your city and be with you, if you find that you can protect him and fulfill your promises to him, otherwise you should return back and leave him, they told the Prophet (PBUH) that he can ask them whatever he and His God want.

The Prophet said: "I pledge you provided that you protect me as you protect your women and children."

They pledged the Prophet (PBUH) but one of them told the Prophet that “we would cut our relation to Jews and would be their enemy but would you leave us and return to your people if your God makes you succeed? The Prophet smiled and told them he was one of them and he would be among them during war and peace.

The Prophet (PBUH) asked them to define 12 leaders from their people; 9 leaders from Banu Khazraj and 3 leaders from Banu Aws.

The Prophet (PBUH) told the leaders that they would be witnesses on their people and he would be witness on his people.

They said that they would protect him with properties and souls and they asked the Prophet about their reward, the Prophet (PBUH) said 'The Heaven'. They said to him to open his hand and they pledged him.

Then, the Prophet (PBUH) said to them to return to their camels. They returned and slept till the morning but when they waked up, Qurayshi people came to them to threaten them saying that they were told that they came to Mecca to get Muhammad out and pledge him to launch war against them and they hated to launch a war against them. The polytheist people answered them denying and swearing that they did not.

The prophet (PBUH) asked his companions to get out to Medina, so they went out. The first one to Migrate from the companions of the Prophet (PBUH) was Abu Salama who migrated to Medina one year before the pledge of Aqaba; he came to mecca from Abyssinia but Quraysh hurt him much so he went out to Medina after he knew that there were who converted to Islam.

Then, 'Amer ibn Rabi'a together with his wife Laila bint Abu Hathma were the first who reached Medina after Abu Salama. Companions of the Prophet (PBUH) reached Medina one by one, but the Prophet was still in Mecca till he was allowed to get out to Medina (Migration). Those who stayed in Mecca were tortured and put in prison till they abandon their conversion to Islam except Ali ibn Abu Talib and Abu Bakr.

Abu Bakr asked the Prophet (PBUH) many times to let him migrate to Medina but the Prophet (PBUH) told him to wait and that he would have a companion while he was migrating.

When Quraysh found that the Prophet (PBUH) became having companions from another country and knew that his companions went out to Medina and stayed there, and the Prophet was about to migrate to them, they gathered in Dar Annadwa to consider his matter.

CHAPTER 6

Tale of what had occurred during the years of migration

Tale of what had occurred during the 1st Hijri Year

It is the 14th year of his prophethood (PBUH); it is 34th year of the rule of Khosrow Pruviz and it is the 9th year of the rule of Heraclius.

The first month of this year is Muharram while the Prophet (PBUH) was staying in Mecca and he had not been out yet. The Prophet commended the companions to get out from Mecca to Medina one by one in Muharram and some of them went out in Dhu Alhijjah. Disbelievers of Quraysh were very interested in the matter of the Prophet (PBUH) and they met in Dar Annadwa, house of Qusai ibn Kilab, to decide what they were doing.

It is said that when they gathered in Dar Annadwa, house of Qusai ibn Kilab, to decide what they would do, Satan came to them in the form of an old man. He told them that he was an old man from Najd wanted to offer his advice and opinion when he listened about their meeting.

The Qurayshi nobility of each tribe were gathered in Dar Annadwa together with some people who were not from Quraysh. Some of them said that this man had a great position and they feared that he would get higher position with the help of others who followed him, so they discussed his matter to decide what they would do.

One of them said to put him in an iron cage till death.

The old man from Najd said: "I do not so support, if you imprisoned him, his companions and people will come and release him".

One of them said: "Let's get him out from our land".

The old man from Najd said: "I do not so support. Did not you see his good speech and logic; and the effect of his sayings on people minds? If you did that, he might go to another place and control its people because of his saying and speech, then he together with those who followed him might march to you defeating you and conquer your land".

Abu Jahl said: "I had an idea. I recommend that you get a young strong man from each tribe, giving them swords to hit him, all at the same time so that he will die and be killed by all the tribes. Then, Banu Abd Manaf will not be able to get revenge from all the Arab tribes and they will agree to get his blood money that we will give to them."

The old man from Najd said: "It is a good opinion, I completely agree; I find no better opinion than this one."

Quraysh nobility concluded their meeting while they decided to fulfill this opinion.

Jibril Came to the Prophet and told him "Do not sleep on your bed." At night, they gathered before the door of the Prophet's house (PBUH). The Prophet (PBUH) asked Ali to sleep on his bed instead of him and not to fear them, they would not hurt him.

At that night, Ali slept on the same place where the Prophet used to sleep and covered with the same blanket whereas the Prophet (PBUH) got out from Mecca and went to the cave. Disbelievers stayed that night watching the house till the morning, then they got in, they saw Ali. They asked Ali about the Prophet (PBUH), Ali answered that he did not know. They went behind the foot traces of the Prophet (PBUH).

It is said that while the Prophet was getting out from his house, he got some aches and spread it on the heads of the disbelievers and they did not see him.

It is said that while the Prophet was getting out from his house, he was reciting to them some verses from Surat Yasin: "Ya, Seen"." يس" (36:1) till the verse: "And We have put before them a barrier and behind them a barrier and covered them, so they do not see"." وَجَعَلْنَا مِن بَيْنِ أَيْدِيهِمْ سَدًّا وَمِنْ خَلْفِهِمْ سَدًّا فَأَغْشَيْنَاهُمْ فَهُمْ لَا يُبْصِرُونَ" (36:9).Then, the Prophet (PBUH) went whenever he wanted. Somebody came to them and asked them what they were waiting for, they replied that they were waiting for Muhammad. The man said to them "Muhammad got out putting dust aches upon on your heads, then he left." They found themselves covered with aches. When they looked at the Prophet's bed (PBUH), they found that there was Ali who was sleeping pretending to be the Prophet (PBUH). In the morning, Ali (May God be pleased with him) waked up while they were watching him. They talked to them-selves concluding that the man's story was true.

Tale how the Prophet (PBUH) and Abu Bakr went to the Cave.

'Aisha narrated that: "One day while we were sitting in our house at midday, someone said to Abu Bakr, "Here is the Prophet (PBUH), coming with his head and a part of his face covered with a cloth-covering at an hour he never used to come to us." Abu Bakr said, "Let my father and mother be sacrificed for you, (O Prophet)! An urgent matter must have brought you here at this hour." The Prophet (PBUH) came and asked the permission to enter, and he was allowed. The Prophet (PBUH) entered and said to Abu Bakr, "Let those who are with you, go out." Abu Bakr replied, "(There is no stranger); they are your family. Let my father be sacrificed for you, O God's Apostle!" The Prophet (PBUH) said, "I have been allowed to leave (Mecca)." Abu Bakr said, "I shall accompany you, O prophet of God (PBUH), Let my father be sacrificed for you!" The Prophet (PBUH) said, "Yes," Abu Bakr said, 'O Prophet (PBUH)! Let my father be sacrificed for you. Take one of these two she camels of mine" The Prophet (PBUH) said. I will take it only after paying its price." So we prepared their baggage and put their journey food in a leather bag. And Asma' bint Abu Bakr cut a piece of her girdle and tied the mouth of the leather bag with it. Then the Prophet (PBUH) and Abu Bakr went to a cave in a mountain called Thour and remained there for three nights.

'Abdullah ibn Abu Bakr who was intelligent and a sagacious youth, used to stay (with them) over night. He used to leave them before day break so that in the morning he would be with Quraysh as if he had spent the night in Mecca. He would keep in mind any plot made against them, and when it became dark he would go and inform them of it. 'Amir ibn Fuhaira, the freed slave of Abu Bakr, used to bring the milk sheep of his master, Abu Bakr to them a little while after nightfall in order to rest the sheep there. So they always had fresh milk at night, the milk of their sheep, and the milk which they warmed by throwing heated stones in it. 'Amir ibn Fuhaira would then call the herd away when it was still dark (before daybreak). He did the same on each of those three nights. The Prophet (PBUH) and Abu Bakr had hired a man from the tribe of Banu Addail from the family of Banu Abd ibn Adi as an expert guide, and he was in alliance with the family of Al'as ibn Wail Assahmi and he was on the religion of the infidels of Quraysh. The Prophet (PBUH) and Abu Bakr trusted him and gave him their two she-camels and took his promise to bring their two she camels to the cave of the mountain of Thaur in the morning after three nights later".

It is narrated that the Prophet stayed in the house of Abu Bakr till the night, then, they went out to the Cave three nights before the end of Safar.

Asma' bint Abu Bakr said: "When they went out, some people of Quraysh, among them was Abu Jahl, came to us, they asked about Abu Bakr, she answered that she did not know where her father was?" Abu Jahl slapped her on her face powerfully to the extent that her earring fell, then they left.

It is said that Abu Bakr took all his money with him and he left nothing for his family when the Prophet (PBUH) got out together with Abu Bakr.

Tale of their stay in the Cave

It is narrated that Anas said that Abu Bakr narrated to him: "While we were in the cave, I said to the Prophet (PBUH): 'If one of them were to look down at his feet, then he would see us under his feet.' So he said: 'O Abu Bakr! What do you think about two, the third of whom is God?'".

It is said that Abu Bakr entered the Cave first, he cut his clothes and blocked each hole or tunnel except one who blocked by his feet, then, he entered then the Prophet (PBUH) entered who asked about his clothes, Abu Bakr told him about what he did. The Prophet (PBUH) raised his hand to the sky and supplicated to God that Abu Bakr will be in the same position of the Prophet (PBUH) in the Heaven.

Quraysh sought Muhammad eagerly till they reached the Cave mouth but they saw that there was a spider web on its opining and they left. Abu Bakr trembled with fear at the sound of the advancing steps of the trackers but Muhammad assured him they were safe as God was with them.

It is said that the Prophet (PBUH) went out from the Cave at Thursday's night on 1st Rabi' I.

Tale of what had occurred while he was on his way (PBUH) to Medina

And (when they set out), 'Amir ibn Fuhaira and the guide went along with them and the guide led them along the sea-shore.

It is narrated that Abu Bakr told that while they went out on their way to Medina (migration), there was nobody could reach them except Suraqa ibn Malik who managed to pursue their footprints. Abu Bakr wept but the Prophet (PBUH) said to him "Do not grieve; indeed God is with us"."لا تَحْزَنْ إِنَّ اللَّـهَ مَعَنَا" (9:40).

Quraysh had announced a reward of 100 camels for anyone who tracked Muhammad and Abu Bakr.

Suraqa was seduced. Suraqa ibn Malik was a clever and patient tracker who followed people upon their footprints on the sand, the excreta of the camels and horses. He asked his slave woman to saddle securely his agile mare and lead her well away from Mecca while he slipped out the back door of his house so that no one would know what he was about to do.

He easily tracked down the two-man caravan of Muhammad on its journey to Medina, but as soon as he caught sight of them, his mare got stuck in the sand, and nothing could rescue her. The Prophet and Abu Bakr were visible by his arrow, but as he lifted his bow to shoot them, his hands got paralyzed. He cried out, ‘O Muhammad, pray for me in order that my pony could get out of this. I promise, I will go back over and give up the pursuit.’

Muhammad prayed, and Suraqa's mare freed herself from the sand. For the size of the reward, Suraqa unfulfilled his word and resumed pursuit of the Prophet and his companion. As he approached Muhammad, the mare got stuck into the sand again. Suraqa again prayed: ‘O Prophet, if I was released again, I would surrender and return to Mecca, never to pursue you. I would deter even others from pursuing you.’

Muhammad prayed again, and the mare again freed herself. Suraqa then declared that Muhammad’s religion would prevail one day and requested Muhammad to hand him a written promise that he would be honored whenever Muhammad became the head of the Islamic state. Abu Bakr wrote the promise at the request of Muhammad on a bone and gave it to Suraqa.

Suraqa encountered several groups of Quraysh who were looking for Muhammad and persuaded them to get back to Mecca as he had found no trace on the route to Medina. The only person whom he told of his encounter was Abu Jahl, who rebuked him for his timidity.

Also, they met Buraydah ibn Alhusayb on their way to Medina

While the Prophet (PBUH) and Abu Bakr were on their way to Medina, Buraydah together with 70 riders from Banu Sahm went out to meet the Prophet. When Buraydah met the prophet (PBUH) and knew that he was the Messenger of God, He said: "I bear witness that there is none worthy of worship except God, I bear witness that Muhammad is the Messenger God." All those who with him converted to Islam.

In the morning, he recommended for the Prophet (PBUH) that he had to raise a flag and asked him to be his guest but the Prophet said that the camel was following an order.

It is said that during the migration, the prophet Muhammad came to halt near the tent of Umm Ma'bad she was a very old lady. Abu Bakr, the prophet's companion wanted to get milk from a goat but he found out that the goat could not even give a drop of milk. It is reported that the Prophet (PBUH) had touched the goat's udder and the goat gave copious amount of milk from which the migrating party and Umm Ma'bad refreshed. When her husband returned and found the milk, he asked her about it and she answered that there was a blessed man passed by her and told him what happened. He said: "I think, he may be the man that Quraysh wants". He asked her to describe the Prophet (PBUH), she did. He said: "O, I swear to God that he was the man of Quraysh, if I was here, I would go with him, I will follow him as long as I can.

Tale of how Medina people met the Prophet (PBUH) and how he entered it.

It is said that when people of Medina knew that the Prophet (PBUH) got out from Mecca, they went out to Alharra (volcanic and stony region) every day till the noon. Once, a Jewish man saw the Prophet and cried 'O Arabs, this is the man whom you are waiting' . They went out to Alharra to meet him but the Prophet (PBUH) turned to the right, where Banu Amr ibn ‘Awf, they are people of Quba.

The Prophet (PBUH) reached Medina on Monday 12th of Rabi' I.

It is narrated that Abu Bakr said: "we (the Prophet and Abu Bakr) came to Medina during the night and the people began to contend as to where the Prophet (PBUH) should reside and he encamped in the tribe of Najar who were related to 'Abdulmutalib from the side of mother. The Prophet (PBUH) honored them, then people climbed upon house-top and women did the same and boys scattered in the way, and they were all crying: Muhammad, Messenger of God, Muhammad, Messenger of God.

Tale of the Place where the Prophet (PBUH) resided when he reached Medina

He stayed his first night in Medina with Banu Al Najar; the maternal uncles of Abdulmutalib

Tale of the joy of Medina's people with his coming (PBUH)

Tale of some events

When the Prophet (PBUH) came, Abyssinians played with spears describing their joy and pleasure for the arrival of the Prophet (PBUH)

It is said that the Prophet resided with Kolthum ibn Alhadm and some said he was Sa'd ibn Khaithamah.

It is said that Abu Bakr resided with Khubaib ibn Isaf.

Ali ibn Abu Talib stayed in Mecca for three days till he handed the deposits and the trusts that were with the Prophet (PBUH), then he went out after the Prophet (PBUH).

The Prophet (PBUH) stayed with Banu 'Awf in Quba on Monday, Tuesday, Wednesday and Thursday and he went out on Friday.

It is said that he stayed for more than 10 days.

It is said that he went out from Quba on Friday and went to medina where he met with Banu Salem; it was the first gathering in Islam, where the Prophet (PBUH) delivered a speech.

The Prophet (PBUH) rode his camel and let it go, when he (PBUH) was passing by a house of the Ansar, they invited him to stay at. The Prophet (PBUH) replied: "Let it go, it was commended", till he stopped at the place of his today mosque. Then, the Prophet stayed with Abu Ayyub Alansari (Khalid ibn Zaid ibn Kulayb).

The Prophet (PBUH) asked about the owner of that place, Mu'az said that it was owned by two orphans and he would give them money till they were pleased. The Prophet commended building his mosque and he stayed with Abu Ayyub till he finished building his mosque and houses.

'Aisha narrated: The Prophet (PBUH) stayed with Banu 'Amr ibn 'Auf for ten nights and established the mosque (mosque of Quba). The Prophet (PBUH) prayed in it and then mounted his she-camel and proceeded on, accompanied by the people till his she-camel knelt down at the place of the Mosque of the Prophet (PBUH) at Medina. Some Muslims used to pray there in those days, and that place was a yard for drying dates belonging to Suhail and Sahl, the orphan boys who were under the guardianship of 'Asad ibn Zurara. When his she-camel knelt down, The Prophet (PBUH) said, "This place, God willing, will be our abiding place." The Prophet (PBUH) then called the two boys and told them to suggest a price for that yard so that he might take it as a mosque. The two boys said, "No, but we will give it as a gift, O The Prophet (PBUH)!" The Prophet (PBUH) then built a mosque there. The Prophet (PBUH) himself started carrying unburnt bricks for its building and while doing so, he was saying "This load is better than the load of Khaibar, for it is more pious in the Sight of God and purer and better rewardable." He was also saying, "O God! The actual reward is the reward in the Hereafter, so bestow Your Mercy on the Ansar and the Emigrants."

A wolf talked outside Medina telling about the Prophet (PBUH)

Abu Huraira narrated: "I heard God's Messenger (PBUH) said, "Whilst a shepherd was amongst his sheep, a wolf attacked them and took away a sheep. The shepherd chased it and got that sheep freed from the wolf. The wolf turned towards the shepherd and said, 'Who will guard the sheep on the day of wild animals when it will have no shepherd except myself?"

The man said, 'O God, I did not see a wolf is talking except what I saw today.' The man was one of Jews and he went to the Prophet (PBUH) and told him about what had happened, the Prophet (PBUH) believed what he said.

Increasing the prayers for non-travelers

'Aisha (The mother of believers) narrated: God order the prayer when He ordered it, it was two prostrations only in every prayer both when in residence or on journey. Then the prayers offered on journey remained the same, but the prostrations of the prayers for non-travelers were increased.

Having sexual intercourse (PBUH) with 'Aisha (May God pleased with her)

In this year: The Prophet (PBUH) had sexual intercourse with 'Aisha (May God be pleased with her) in Shawal, it is said that it was in the second year, He got married to her three years before migration. This event was occurred in the house of Abu Bakr (May God be pleased with him).

The Prophet (PBUH) sent somebody to fetch his daughters and wife

In this year, the Prophet (PBUH) sent Zaid ibn Haritha and Abu Rafi' to his daughters and wife to take them from Mecca to Medina.

When Abdullah ibn Uraiket returned to Mecca, he told Abdullah ibn Abu Bakr the place of his father. Abdullah went out to Medina together with the children of his father, Talha ibn 'Ubaid and Umm Rumman – Mother of 'Aisha.

Establishing the bond of brotherhood between the Quraysh (Migrants) and the Ansar

Anas ibn Malik reported God's Messenger (PBUH) saying: There is no alliance (hilf) of brotherhood in Islam. Anas said: God's Messenger (PBUH) established the bond of fraternity between Quraysh and Ansar in his home.

It is said that when the Prophet (PBUH) came to Medina, he established the bond of brotherhood between the migrants (Quraysh) and the Ansar regarding rights and inheritance.

It is said that they were 90 men: 45 men from the Ansar and 45 men from Quraysh.

It is said that they were 100 men: 50 men from the Ansar and 50 men from Quraysh.

This event had occurred before battle of Badr as after the battle, God, Exalted and Glorified is He, had revealed: "But those of [blood] relationship are more entitled [to inheritance] in the decree of God"." وَأُولُوا الْأَرْحَامِ بَعْضُهُمْ أَوْلَى بِبَعْضٍ فِي كِتَابِ الله" (8:75).

This verse negated all what occurred before its revelation; the inheritance because of the fraternity bond was stopped and only those of blood relationship (kinship) are entitled of inheritance.

The Prophet (PBUH) commended to fast on the day of 'Ashura

In this year, he (PBUH) found the Jews fasting on the day of 'Ashura.

Ibn 'Abbas reported that When the Messenger of God (PBUH) arrived at Medina and found the Jews performing fast on the day of 'Ashura. The Messenger of God (PBUH) said to them:

"What is the (significance) of this day that you perform fast on?" They said: "It is the day of great (significance) when God delivered Moses and his people, and drowned the Pharaoh and his people, and Moses performed fast out of gratitude and we also perform it. Upon this the Messenger of God (PBUH) said: We are more entitled to this, and we have a closer connection with Moses than you have; so God's Messenger (PBUH) performed fast (on the day of 'Ashura), and gave orders that it should be performed.

Abdullah ibn Salam's conversion to Islam

Abdullah ibn Salam said: “When the Prophet (PBUH) came to Al-Medina, the people rushed to meet him. I came with the people to see him, and when I saw his face clearly, I knew that his face was not the face of a liar. The first thing I heard him say was when he said: ‘O people! Spread (the greeting of) Salam, feed others, uphold the ties of kinship, and pray during the night when people are sleeping, and you will enter Paradise with Salam.”

Abdullah ibn Zayd was taught in a dream how to pronounce the call to prayer

During this year, Abdullah ibn Zayd was taught in a dream how to pronounce the call to prayer and he taught it to Bilal.

ʿAbdullah ibn Zayd reported: When the Messenger of God (PBUH) ordered a bell to be made so that it might be struck to gather the people for prayer, a man carrying a bell in his hand appeared to me while I was asleep. I said; servant of Abdullah, will you sell the bell? He asked; what will you do with it? I replied; we shall use it to call the people to prayer. He said; should I suggest you something better than that. I replied: certainly. Then he told me to say: God is most great, God is most great, God is most great, God is most great. I testify that there is no deity but

God, I testify that Muhammad is the Messenger of God. Come to pray, come to pray; come to salvation; come to salvation. God is most great, God is most great. I testify that there is no deity but God. He then moved backward a few steps and said: when you utter the IQAMAH, you should say: God is most great, God is most great. I testify that there is no deity but God, I testify that Muhammad is the Messenger of God. Come to prayer, come to salvation. The time for prayer has come, the time for prayer has come: God is most great, God is most great. There is no deity but God.

When the morning came, I came to the Messenger of God (May peace be upon him) and informed him of what I had seen in the dream. He said: it is a genuine vision, and he then should use it to call people to prayer, for he has a louder voice than yours. So I got up along with Bilal and began to teach it to him and he used it in making the call to prayer. ‘Umar ibn Alkhattab (May God be pleased with him) heard it while he was in his house and came out trailing his cloak and said: Messenger of God. The Messenger of God (PBUH) said: To God be the praise. "Bilal added the phrase "As-salatu khairum minan-nawm (The prayer is better than sleep)" to the call for the morning prayer, and the Messenger of Allah approved that."

At first, the call for prayer was held by someone who was calling for people and saying 'Assalatu Jame'a' (Gather for the prayer) but when Qibla turned to be to Kaaba, the Prophet (PBUH) wanted another method to call for the prayer.

It is said that the Prophet (PBUH) and Muslims were turning to Jerusalem while they were praying for 16 months before turning to Kaaba.

Thus, based on this narration, the call for prayer initiated during the 2nd Hijri year.

Tale of his brigades (PBUH) in this year

Brigade of Hamza ibn Abdulmutalib

In this year, the Prophet (PBUH) made a white banner for Hamza ibn Abdulmutalib, it was the first banner he (PBUH) made, 7 months after his migration (PBUH) in Ramadan. The Prophet (PBUH) sent Hamza heading 30 men of migrants to intercept camels for Quraysh where he met Abu Jahl together with 300 hundred men. While they were about to fight with each other, Magdi ibn Amr Aljahni stopped them as he was an ally for both parties, so there was not any battle; Abu Jahl returned to Mecca and Hamza returned to Medina.

Brigade of Ubaydah ibn Alharith

In this year, the Prophet (PBUH) made a white banner in Shawwal for Ubaydah ibn Alharith ibn Abdulmutalib and sent him with a party of sixty armed Muhajirun (migrants), to the valley of Rabigh. They were to intercept a Quraysh caravan that was returning from Syria under the protection of Abu Sufyan ibn Harb and 200 armed riders. The Muslim party travelled as far as the wells, where Saad ibn Abu Waqqas shot an arrow at Quraysh. This is known as the first arrow of Islam. Despite this surprise attack, "They did not unsheathe a sword or approach one another," and the Muslims returned empty-handed.

Brigade of Saad ibn Abu Waqqas

Saad ibn Abu Waqqas was sent to Alkhazar in Dulqi'dah and was given a white banner held by Miqdad ibn Amr. He was sent together with 20 men of the migrants to intercept camels (Caravan) for Quraysh. Saad said: "We went on foot, so we were having rest at day and marching at night, till we reached there but we found that the camels passed by the place yesterday, then we returned"

Tale of those who died in this Year

- Asaad ibn Zurarah (Abu Umama)

He went to Mecca and heard about the Prophet (PBUH), so he went to the Prophet (PBUH) as he invited him to Islam. He converted to Islam and was the first to enter Medina as Muslim.

Asaad was one of the twelfth leaders of Aqaba. When Musaab ibn 'Umair returned to Mecca to the Prophet (PBUH), Asaad was the man who led Muslims while they were performing the prayers in the place of the mosque of the Prophet (PBUH) five times a day.

Asaad died before finishing the construction of the Prophet's Mosque (PBUH) and he was buried at Albaqi' and it is said he was the first one to be buried there.

When Asaad died, Banu Alnajar went to the Prophet (PBUH) and asked him to choose a leader for them, the Prophet (PBUH) said to them that they were his maternal uncles and he was from them so he was their leader.

- Albara' ibn Ma'rur ibn Sakhr ibn Khansa' ibn Senan:

He was one of those who were in Aqaba; he was one of 70 men of Ansar who allied the Prophet (PBUH) and he was one of the leaders. He returned to Medina and died a month before the Prophet’s (PBUH) migration to Medina. He was the first leader to die.

- Kulthum ibn Alhadm ibn Imru' Alqais ibn Alharith

He was one of the nobles, an old man. He converted to Islam before the migration of the Prophet (PBUH) to Medina.

Tale of those who died from polytheists

In this year, there were two polytheists died; Al'as ibn Wa'il Assahmi and Walid ibn Almughirah Almakhzoumi.

Tale of what had occurred in the 2nd Hijri year

Events:

Ali ibn Abu Talib married to Fatima (May God be pleased with them) in Safar but they had sexual intercourse in Dhu Alhijjah. Fatima was 18 years when she married to Ali.

Patrol of Alabwa'

It was the first battle that the Prophet (PBUH) participated in and he appointed Saad ibn Ubadah. He went out with Almuhajirun till he reached Alabwa' to seize the carvan of Quraysh. He (PBUH) went after them till he reached Wadan, so it was called Patrol of Waddan, but he met Banu Damrah where they established a peace agreement for mutual cooperation and safety. There was no fighting occurred during this campaign. Then, the Prophet was away from Medina for 15 nights.

Battle of Buwat

The Prophet (PBUH) went out to it in Rabi' I of the 2nd Hijri year. The Banner was held by Saad ibn Mu'adh. The Prophet (PBUH) together with 200 men of Almuhajirun went out to catch the caravan of Quraysh, that were guarded by Ummayyah ibn Khalaf and 100 men from Quraysh till he reached Buwat but there was no fighting as they did not meet each other.

Battle against Kurz ibn Jabur Alfihri

Kurz ibn Jabur Alfihri is a companion of The Prophet (PBUH) but he used to be an enemy. During the Invasion of Safwan, he crackled some grazing cattle belonging to the Muslims. Muhammad (PBUH) together with seventy Muslims went after him till they reached Safwan, at the outskirts of Badr. But Kurz ibn Jabur Alfihri managed to escape. Then they returned to Medina. The Prophet (PBUH) had appointed Zaid ibn Harithah as a leader in Medina, during his absence.

Patrol of Dhul Ushairah

Patrol of Dhul Ushairah occurred in the 2nd Hijri year in Jumada II. This was the 6th caravan expedition and the 3rd ‘Ghazwah’, i.e.: (expedition), Muhammad himself was the commander, it took place about 2 months after the that of Buwaṭ. The Prophet in conjunction with 150-200 Muslim volunteers went out to intercept Quraysh caravan. The Prophet (PBUH) went off till he reached Al'ushayrah, in the valley of Yanbu. He expected to trap that caravan there but he missed the caravan. His banner was carried by Ḥamza ibn Abdulmutalib.

The Prophet left Abu Salamah ibn 'Abd Alasad in charge of Medina while he was away.

This was the same caravan led by Abu Sufyan that the Prophet set out to intercept on its return from Syria two months after Dhul 'Ushayrah expedition, and was the main reason for the break out of the Battle of Badr.

Raid on Nakhla (Brigade of Abdullah ibn Jahsh Alasadi)

It was in Rajab of the 2nd Hijri year. The Prophet (PBUH) dispatched 'Abdullah ibn Jahsh Alasadi to Nakhlah, on the outskirts of Mecca, heading eight migrants with six camels, waiting for the Quraysh and watching what they were doing. Saad ibn Abu Waqqas and Utbah ibn Ghazwan lost a camel that they were taking turns to ride. The camel drifted and went to Buhran, so they went out looking for the escaped camel to Buhran and fell behind the group. They returned to Medina after them.

Changing Qibla towards Kaaba

It is said that Qibla was changed towards Kaaba at noon on Tuesday, 15th of Sha'ban of the 2nd Hijri Year.

It is said that Qibla was changed on 15th Rajab of the 2nd Hijri year.

Others supported that the Prophet (PBUH) turned to Jerusalem for 16 or 17 months and then to Kaaba two months before battle of Badr.

Building of Quba' Mosque

It is said that when Qibla changed to Kaaba, the Prophet (PBUH) came to Quba' Mosque and established its wall in its place of today. The Prophet (PBUH) together with his companions constructed it. It is said that it was a mosque was built upon piety.

Revelation of Ramadan's religious duty of Fasting and Fast-breaking Zakat

This occurred in Sha'ban in that year.

It is narrated that the religious duty of Ramadan Fasting happened a month after changing Qibla direction to Kaaba and 18 months after migration of the Prophet (PBUH), as the Prophet (PBUH) prescribed Fast-breaking Zakat before Zakat upon money. The Messenger of God (PBUH) prescribed that Zakat is payable by slave and freeman, males and females, among the Muslims on closing the fast of Ramadan as one measure of dried dates or one measure of barley. The Prophet (PBUH) ordered the payment of Fast-breaking Zakat before people go out for prayer of Eid.

In this year, Abdullah ibn Alzubayr ibn Al'awwam was born 20 months after migration; he was the first new born in Medina after migration.

Battle of Badr

From that year events was Battle of Badr

It happened at that Friday morning, 17th of Ramadan.

Well of Badr was owned by a man called Badr.

Prior to the battle, the Muslims and the Meccans had engaged in several smaller clashes. Abdullah ibn Jahsh and his party disguised as pilgrims with shaved heads, upon being discovered by a Meccan caravan, decided to strike and kill as many of the caravan as possible, resulting in claiming the life of one of its men, Amr ibn Alhadrami, then they seized its goods and captured two as prisoners. It was the most serious since the killing occurred in the month of Rajab in Badr, however, it was the first extensive engagement between the two forces. Muhammad's well-disciplined forces attacked the Meccan lines, killing several important leaders from Quraysh including the Muslims' enemy Abu Jahl. It was reported in Medina that Abu Sufyan was leading a caravan from Syria to Mecca holding weapons to be used against the Muslims. Muhammad mobilized 313 men and went to Badr to seize the caravan. Meccan spies informed Abu Sufyan about the Muslims arrival, aiming to intercept the caravan; Abu Sufyan changed his way to another to Mecca and sent a message thereto. Consequently Abu Jahl replied to Abu Sufyan's request and mobilzed an army to wage war against the Muslims.

On the other side, Muhammad's forces included Abu Bakr, Umar, Ali, Hamza, Mus`ab ibn `Umair, Azzubair ibn Al'awwam, Ammar ibn Yasir, and Abu Dharr Alghifari. The Muslims also brought seventy camels and two horses, that they either had to walk or fit three - four men per camel. Uthman stayed behind to take care of his sick wife Ruqayyah, the daughter of Muhammad

Many of the nobles of Quraysh, including Amr ibn Hisham, Walid ibn Utba, Shaiba, and Ummayyah ibn Khalaf, joined the Meccan army, some were out to defend their financial interests in the caravan, a few wanted to participate in what was expected to be an effortless victory against the Muslims.

When the word spread and reached the Muslim army concerning the departure of the Meccan army, Muhammad immediately called for a council of war, as there was still some time to withdraw and because many of the troops were recent converts, who had only promised to defend Medina. They would have been within their rights to refuse to go into battle and leave the army.

Then, Abu Bakr gave a short speech, Umar then spoke, expressing similar views to that of Abu Bakr. Later, Miqdad gave a speech encouraging Muhammad, saying, "O Prophet of God! Our hearts are with you and you should act according to the orders given to you by God. By God! We shall not tell you what Banu Israel told Moses. When Moses asked them to perform Jihad they said to him: 'O Moses! You and your Lord should go and perform Jihad and we shall sit here'. Yet, we tell you quite the opposite: Perform Jihad under the auspices of the blessings of God and we are also with you and shall fight." Miqdad's speech pleased

Muhammad who also wanted to know what Ansar thought, as Miqdad was a migrant. Saad ibn Mu'az, one of Ansar, declared, "We have borne witness that you are the Messenger of God. We have pledged to obey you. Wherever you go, we shall follow you. If there is a confrontation with the polytheists, we shall be resolute, supporting you, in war and in peace, we shall be consistently faithful to you." Thus, the Muslims resumed their march towards Badr. The Prophet (PBUH) was pleased and commended them to march towards Badr and arrived before the Meccans.

The Badr wells were located on the gentle slope of the eastern side of a valley called "Yalyal". The western side of the valley was edged by a large hill called 'Aqanqal.

It is said that the Prophet (PBUH) sent some companions to the well of Badr to get some information about the army of Quraysh, they captured two slaves. They took them to the Prophet (PBUH) who posed some questions about number of the army but they did not know anything about this matter. The Prophet (PBUH) asked them about how many camels they ate per day, they answered that they ate 9 to 10 camels. According to that, the Prophet (PBUH) concluded that the army was about 900 to 1000 man.

When Quraysh fighters reached Juhfah, south of Badr, they got a message from Abu Sufyan telling them that the caravan was at safe behind them, and that they could return to Mecca. Thus, Abu Jahl wanted to carry on, but several of the present clans, as well as Banu Zuhrah and Banu Adi, hastily returned. Banu Hashim tribe wanted to depart, but was threatened by Abu Jahl, so as to stay. Notwithstanding these losses, Abu Jahl was still determined to fight, saying: "We will not go home until we reach Badr." During this period, Abu Sufyan and several other men from the caravan joined up the main army.

When the Muslim army arrived, Muhammad at the outset chose to form his army at the first well he faced. Hubab ibn Al-mundhir, however, asked him if this choice was out of divine instruction or Muhammad's own opinion. Muhammad said it is his own suggestion, Hubab indicated that the Muslims must occupy the nearest well to Quraysh army, and close off the others. Jibril descended and told the Prophet (PBUH) that it was a good opinion, so Muhammad agreed to this decision and moved right away.

Quraysh marched to the valley of Badr. There were heavy rains and they struggled to move with their horses and camels up the hill of Aqanqal. After they descended from Aqanqal, they put up another camp inside the valley. While they rested, they sent out an emissary, Umayr ibn Wahb to identify the Muslim lines. Umayr reported that Muhammad's army was of a small size, and that there were no other Muslim forces which might join the battle. He also foresaw heavy casualties for Quraysh in the event of an attack. This dispirited Quraysh and set off another round of backbiting among the Qurayshi leadership. According to Arab traditions Amr ibn Hisham suppressed the remaining dissent by appealing to Quraysh's sense of honor and requiring that they fulfill their blood vengeance

Alaswad ibn Abd Alasad Almakhzoumi departed to reach the well but Hamza managed to kill him. Then, Utbah and Shaybah ibn Rabu'ah and his son Alwalid and asked for sword fighting. So, Hamza approached forward and called on Ubayda and Ali to join him. The Muslims forwarded the Meccan champions in a three-on-three. The first fight was between Ali and Walid ibn Utba; Ali killed his opponent. After the fight between Ali and Walid, Hamza fought with Utba ibn Rabu'ah, and Ubayda struggled Shaybah ibn Rabu'ah. Hamza killed Utbah; however, Ubayda was seriously wounded by Shaybah. Ali killed Shaybah. Ali and Hamza then carried Ubayda back into the Muslim lines, then he died.

Consequently, both armies started bombarding each other with arrows. Some Muslims and an unspecified number of Quraysh fighters were killed. Before the battle, the Prophet (PBUH) had given orders for the Muslims to attack initially with their ranged weapons and only afterwards advance to engage the Quraysh with weapons. The prophet (PBUH) worked on establishing the lines and he was supplicating to God to achieve What God, Exalted is He, promised.

Then, the Prophet yield and said: 'O Abu Bakr, the victory of God is coming!" The Prophet (PBUH) threw a handful of pebbles at the Meccans in what was probably a traditional Arabian act while shouting "Defaced be those faces!"

There were many polytheists who were killed and captivated.

Killed and captivated polytheists

Consequently, 70 polytheists were killed and 70 other were captivated.

It has been narrated by Umar ibn Alkhattab: "When it was the day on which the Battle of Badr was fought, the Messenger of God (PBUH) cast a glance at the infidels, and they were one thousand while his own Companions were three hundred and nineteen. The Prophet (PBUH) turned his face towards the Qibla. Then he stretched his hands and began his supplication to his Lord: "O God, accomplish for me what Thou hast promised to me. O God, bring about what Thou hast promised to me. O God, if this small band of Muslims is destroyed. Thou will not be worshipped on this earth." He continued his supplication to his Lord, stretching his hands, facing the Qibla, until his mantle slipped down from his shoulders. So Abu Bakr came to him, picked up his mantle and put it on his shoulders. Then he embraced him from behind and said: Prophet of God, this prayer of yours to your

Lord will suffice you, and He will fulfill for you what He has promised you. So God, the Glorious and Exalted, revealed (the Qur'anic verse): "[Remember] when you asked help of your Lord, and He answered you, "Indeed, I will reinforce you with a thousand from the angels, following one another"." إِذْ تَسْتَغِيثُونَ رَبَّكُمْ فَاسْتَجَابَ لَكُمْ أَنِّي مُمِدُّكُم بِأَلْفٍ مِّنَ الْمَلَائِكَةِ مُرْدِفِينَ" (8:9). This was the help from the third heaven. The Muslims that day (i.e. the day of the Battle of Badr) killed seventy persons and captured seventy."

The Messenger of God (PBUH) said to Abu Bakr and `Umar (God be pleased with them): "What is your opinion about these captives?" Abu Bakr said: "They are our kith and kin. I think you should release them after getting from them a payment. This will be a source of power to us against the infidels. It is quite possible that God may guide them to Islam." Then the Messenger of God (PBUH) said: "What is your opinion, Ibn Alkhattab?" He said: "Messenger of God, I do not agree with Abu Bakr. I see that you should hand them over to us so that we may cut off their heads. Hand over `Aqil to `Ali that he may execute him, and hand over such and such relative to me that I may cut off his head. They are leaders of the disbelievers."

The Messenger of God (PBUH) approved the opinion of Abu Bakr and did not approve what I said. The next day when I came to the Messenger of God (PBUH), I found that both he and Abu

Bakr were sitting shedding tears, I said: "Messenger of God, why are you and your Companion shedding tears? Tell me the reason. For I will weep, or I will at least pretend to weep in sympathy with you. The Messenger of God (PBUH) said: I weep for what has happened to your companions for taking ransom (from the prisoners). I was shown the torture to which they were subjected. It was brought to me as close as this tree. (He pointed to a tree close to him.) Then God, Exalted is He, has revealed the verses: "It is not for a prophet to have captives [of war] until he inflicts a massacre [upon God's enemies] in the land. Some Muslims desire the commodities of this world, but God desires [for you] the Hereafter. And God is Exalted in Might and Wise. If not for a decree from God that preceded, you would have been touched for what you took by a great punishment"." "مَا كَانَ لِنَبِيٍّ أَن يَكُونَ لَهُ أَسْرَىٰ حَتَّىٰ يُثْخِنَ فِي الْأَرْضِ تُرِيدُونَ عَرَضَ الدُّنْيَا وَاللَّـهُ يُرِيدُ الْآخِرَةَ وَاللَّـهُ عَزِيزٌ حَكِيمٌ. لَّوْلَا كِتَابٌ مِّنَ اللَّـهِ سَبَقَ لَمَسَّكُمْ فِيمَا أَخَذْتُمْ عَذَابٌ عَظِيمٌ" (9:67-68).

Tale of Abu Jahl killing

`Abd Alrahman ibn 'Awf narrated: "While I was standing in the row on the day (of the battle) of Badr, I looked to my right and my left and saw two young Ansari boys, and I wished I had been stronger than them. One of them called my attention saying, "O Uncle! Do you know Abu Jahl?" I said, "Yes, What do you want from him, O my nephew?" He said, "I have been informed that he abuses God's Messenger (PBUH). By Him in Whose Hands my life is, if I should see him, then my body will not leave his body till either of us meet his fate." I was astonished at that talk. Then the other boy called my attention saying the same as the other had said. After a while I saw Abu Jahl walking amongst the people. I said (to the boys), "Look! This is the man you asked me about." So, both of them attacked him with their swords and struck him to death and returned to God'S Prophet to inform him of that. God's Messenger (PBUH) asked, "Which of you has killed him?" Each of them said, "I Have killed him." God's Messenger (PBUH) asked, "Have you cleaned your swords?" They said, "No." He then looked at their swords and said, "No doubt, you both have killed him and the spoils of the deceased will be given to Mu`adh ibn `Amr ibn Aljamuh." The two boys were Mu`adh ibn 'Afra and Mu`adh ibn `Amr ibn Aljamuh."

Abu Jahl was killed while he was 70 years old.

Tale of Angels' Descent

Scholars said that there were winds that blew on the day of Badr; the first was by Jibril and thousand angels with the Prophet (PBUH); the second was by Michael and thousand angels on the right of the Prophet (PBUH); and the third was by Israfil and thousand angels on the left of the Prophet (PBUH).

Angels fought during Badr only and they attended other battles but without fighting.

There were many narrations from those people who witnessed battle of Badr who said that there were others who fought with them during the battle and they did not see them but they felt their existence.

Abu Zumail said that a hadith was narrated to him by Ibn `Abbas who said: While on that day a Muslim was chasing a disbeliever who was going ahead of him, he heard over him the swishing of the whip and the voice of the rider saying: Go ahead, Haizum! He glanced at the polytheist who had (now) fallen down on his back. When he looked at him (carefully he found that) there was a scar on his nose and his face was torn as if it had been lashed with a whip, and had turned green with its poison. An Ansari came to the Messenger of God (PBUH) and related this (event) to him. He said: You have told the truth. This was the help from the third heaven."

Abu Talha narrated: On the day of Badr, the Prophet (PBUH) ordered that the corpses of twenty four leaders of Quraysh should be thrown into one of the dirty dry wells of Badr. It was a habit of the Prophet (PBUH) that whenever he conquered some people, he used to stay at the battle-field for three nights. So, on the third day of the battle of Badr, he ordered that his she-camel be saddled, then he set out, and his companions followed him, saying: "Definitely he (i.e. the Prophet) is proceeding for some great purpose." When he halted at the edge of the well, he addressed the corpses of the Quraysh infidels by their names and their fathers' names, "O so-and-so, son of so-and-so and O so-and-so, son of so-and so! Would it have pleased you if you had obeyed God and His Prophet? We have found true what our Lord promised us. Have you too found true what your lord promised you? "`Umar said, "O God's Messenger (PBUH)! You are speaking to bodies that have no souls!" God's Messenger (PBUH) said, "By Him in Whose Hand Muhammad's soul is, you do not hear, what I say better than they do." (Qatada said, "God brought them to life (again) to let them hear him, to reproach them, take revenge over them and to cause them to feel remorseful and regretful."

The Prophet (PBUH) said that each one was granted the booty he collected but when he ordered the booty to be collected and asked about who collected it, some introduced themselves, some fighters said: "If we were not there, you could not collect it and those who were guarding the Prophet (PBUH) said: "You are not the ones to deserve the booty but we who deserve it"

So, when people disagreed regarding the booty distribution, God has revealed that it was for the Prophet (PBUH), then, the Prophet equally distributed it over Muslims.

Then, the Prophet (PBUH) sent Abdullah ibn Rawahah as a bringer for good tiding for people of the uphill and sent Zaid ibn Haritha to people of the downhill.

Usama ibn Zaid said that the news came to them when they were burying Ruqayyah, daughter of the Prophet (PBUH), wife of Uthman ibn 'Affan.

Then, when the Prophet was on his way to Medina, he divided and distributed the booty.

When Muslims met him (PBUH), they congratulated him with this victory.

The Prophet (PBUH) entered Medina one day before the captives but he commended that the captives must be treated well.

Chapter

The first one to give the bad tiding to Meccans was Alhaisaman ibn Abdullah ibn Iyas.

Quraysh mourned for their killed men but they decided not to show lest Muhammad and his followers (PBUH) should rejoice for their misfortune.

The Prophet (PBUH) said to his uncle Abbas: "Redeem yourself, your nephew Uqaile ibn Abu Talib, Nawfal ibn Alharith and your ally Utbah ibn Amr, you are a rich man". Abbas said that he did not own money so the Prophet (PBUH) told him about the money he left for his wife to divide it among his children. When Abbas was told about the money he left and no one knew about it except his wife, he declared that Muhammad was the Messenger of God and converted to Islam and he redeemed himself and others.

Abu Al'as ibn Alrabu', husband of Zainab, daughter of the Prophet (PBUH), was one of the captives, so Zainab sent a necklace that her mother Khadija gave her when she married to Al'as, The Prophet (PBUH) felt sympathy for her and told his companions to give her necklace back together with freeing her captive but the Prophet (PBUH) stipulated that Al'as would let Zainab come to the Prophet (PBUH) as he prevented her from migrating, followng her father as she believed in him. When Al'as returned to Mecca and wanted to get Zainab out from Mecca to go to her father, Abu Sufyan prevented him and told him to send her later Then, Al'as sent her to her father (PBUH) in secret and he stayed in Mecca.

Before conquer of Mecca, Al'as went out for trading but he was caught by a brigade that seized his camels but he managed to flee. He managed to reach Zainab under darkness to save him. In the morning, Zainab cried and said that she saved and protected Al'as, the Prophet (PBUH) entered to his daughter and said to her to be generous to him but he was unlawful to her. The Prophet said to the brigade: "If you are generous, you may give what you took from him or it will be booty for you." They agreed to give him back his camels.

Al'as returned to Mecca and gave people their money back and he said "I bear witness that there is no deity but God and Muhammad is His servant and messenger.

Tale of the favor of those who fought during battle of Badr

Rifa'ah ibn Rafi' Azzuraqi (May God be pleased with him), he was a man of the Badr warriors, who said: "Jibril came to the Prophet (PBUH) and asked him: "How do you estimate among you those who participated in the battle of Badr?" He replied, "They were the best of Muslims" (or he may have said something similar to that). Jibril said: "The same is the case with the angels who were at Badr."

It is narrated by Ali that the Prophet (PBUH) said: "Who knows, perhaps God has already looked at Badr warriors and said, 'Do whatever you like, for I have forgiven you."

Tale of the number of Badr warriors

Al-Bara' narrated that: "We used to say that the participants of Badr on the Day of Badr were like the number of companions of Talut, three hundred and thirteen men."

Ibn 'Abbas said: It has been narrated on the authority of `Umar ibn Alkhattab who said: "When it was the day on which the Battle of Badr was fought, the Messenger of God (PBUH) cast a glance at the infidels, and they were one thousand while his own Companions were three hundred and nineteen."

The banner of the Prophet (PBUH) was held by Ali ibn Abu Talib and the banner of Ansar was held by Saad ibn 'Ubadah.

It is said that number of the companions of the Prophet (PBUH) at the battle of Badr were 313 or 314 men; 270 men from Ansar.

It is said that the number of Muhajirun from Quraysh and their allies and slaves were 83 men and some said they were 85 men.

It is said that the number of warriors of Badr from Al'aws were 63 men and others said they were 61 men.

It is said that the number of warriors of Badr from Khazraj were 175 men and others said they were 170 men.

All warriors whether they were from Almuhajirun or Ansar who participated in the battle of Badr were 313 men, some said they were 314 men and others said they were 316 men.

Eight men were absent on the day of Badr but the Prophet (PBUH) gave them their share in the booty as if they participated in the fighting.

Chapter

On the same day where the Prophet (PBUH) was victorious in the battle of Badr, Persians fought against the Byzantines while the Byzantines defeated the Persians.

Sa'eed ibn Jubair narrated regarding the saying of God, Exalted is He: "Alif, Lam, Meem. The Byzantines have been defeated. In the nearest land But they, after their defeat, will overcome"." "الم.غُلِبَتِ الرُّومُ، فِي أَدْنَى الْأَرْضِ وَهُم مِّن بَعْدِ غَلَبِهِمْ سَيَغْلِبُونَ" (30:1-3) He said: "The polytheists wanted the Persians to be victorious over the Byzantines because they too were people who worshiped idols, while the Muslims wanted the Byzantines to be victorious over the Persians because they were people of the Book". He said: "Afterwards the Byzantines have been victorious." Exalted is He says: "And that day the believers will rejoice In the victory of God. He gives victory to whom He wills"." "وَيَوْمَئِذٍ يَفْرَحُ الْمُؤْمِنُونَ بِنَصْرِ اللَّـهِ، يَنصُرُ مَن يَشَاءُ" (30:4-5).

Brigade of 'Umair ibn 'Udai

It is one of the events in this year; it was to Asma bint Marawan in Ramadan in the 2nd Hijri year. She was a female Arab tribeswoman who lived in Medina in the 7th-century. She was known for ridiculing the people of Medina for obeying a chief not of their own kind and she used to ridicule Islam. He crept into her room in the dark of night where she was sleeping with her five children, with her infant child close to her heart. Umayr removed the child from Asma's breast and put his sword in her chest.

Brigade of Salem ibn 'Umair

Also, it was sent to Abu 'Afak, the Jewish poet, in Shawal. As an elderly man, Abu 'Afak Arwan wrote a politically charged poem against Muhammad and his supporters. Muhammad then allegedly called for Abu 'Afak's death, and Salim ibn Umair killed him.

The stories of both Asma bint Marwan and Abu Afak are graded as weak and fabricated by the majority of Islamic scholars in history.

Invasion of Banu Qaynuqa

The Banu Qaynuqa was a Jewish tribe expelled by the Islamic prophet Muhammad for breaking the treaty known as the Constitution of Medina. When the Prophet (PBUH) came to Medina, he concluded a treaty with them as they would not help others against the Prophet (PBUH). When the Prophet (PBUH) won the Battle of Badr, they envied him, then they breached their pact with him.

The Prophet (PBUH) had gathered the Jews of Banu Qaynuqa and he warned them that they would be defeated like Quraysh after they knew that he was a prophet sent by God. They told him (PBUH) that they were not like his people whom he defeated and if they fought him, he would find strong and severe people.

Thus, the Prophet (PBUH) went out in the middle of Shawal to fight them, the banner was held by Hamza, he left Abu Lubabh in the charge of Medina. They hid in their forts, so the Prophet

(PBUH) sieged them for 15 days till they surrendered for the Prophet (PBUH). They left Medina and the Prophet won the booty; it was the second booty after Badr's, then he returned to Medina.

Some scholars see that the battle of Banu Qaynuqa was in the 3rd Hijri year.

In the same year, the Prophet (PBUH) together with his companions went out and performed Eid's prayer. Also, He (PBUH) together with his rich companions sacrificed; it was the first Eid, then.

Tale of those who died in this year

- Haritha ibn Suraqa

Anas ibn Malik narrated that: Um Arrubai' bint Albara', the mother of Haritha ibn Suraqa came to the Prophet (PBUH) and said, "O God's Prophet! Will you tell me about Haritha?" Haritha has been killed (i.e. martyred) on the day of Badr with an arrow thrown by an unidentified person. She added, "If he is in the Heaven, I will be patient; otherwise, I will weep bitterly for him." He said, "O mother of Haritha! There are Gardens in the Heaven and your son got the Firdaus Ala'la (i.e. the best place in the Heaven).

- Ruqayyah, the Prophet's daughter:

She married to Uttba ibn Abu Lahab before the prophecy of Muhammad. However, when Muhammad was sent as a prophet, Abu Lahab ordered his son to leave her, and he did not have sexual intercourse with her. She then married to Uthman, whom she migrated with to Abyssinia. She had one abortion but then God gifted her with a son, named Abdullah. She got sick during the preparations to Badr, thus Uthman was absent, she died in Ramadan.

- Saad ibn Khaithama

Saad ibn Khaithama was one of the 12 leaders who witnessed the last pledge of Aqaba together with 70 men. When the Prophet (PBUH) invited people to get out for battle of Badr, he went out to the battle and he was killed there.

- Saad ibn Malik ibn Khalaf ibn Tha'labah ibn Haritha

He was ready to get out to Badr but he died, the Prophet (PBUH) allowed him a share and reward.

- Safwan ibn Baida' ibn Wahb

He was killed in battle of Badr but some said that he was not.

- 'Aqil ibn Albakeer ibn 'Abd Yalil ibn Nashib

'Aqil converted to Islam in Dar Alarqam, all Banu Albakeer got out of Mecca to Medina. He was killed during Badr while he was 34 years, he was killed by Malik ibn Zuhair Algashmi.

- Ubaydah ibn Alharith ibn Abdulmutalib ibn Abd Manaf ibn Qusayy

He was older than the Prophet (PBUH) by 10 years, he converted to Islam before entering the Prophet (PBUH) into Dar Alarqam. He was killed on the day of Badr by Shaybah ibn Rabu'ah. He was 63 when he was killed.

- 'Umair ibn Alhamam

He was the first to be killed from Ansar, he was killed by Khalid ibn Ala'lam. The Prophet (PBUH) had associated him a brother to 'Ubaydah ibn Alharith, they were all killed in Badr.

Anas ibn Malik reported Messenger of God (PBUH) saying: "Get up to enter Paradise which is equal in width to the heavens and the earth." 'Umair ibn Alhumam al-Ansari said: "Messenger of God, is Paradise equal in extent to the heavens and the earth?" He said: "Yes." 'Umair said: "My goodness!" The Messenger of God (PBUH) asked him: "What prompted you to utter these words (i. e. my goodness! ')?" He said: "Messenger of God, nothing but the desire that I be among its residents." He took out dates from his bag and began to eat them. Then he said: "If I were to live until I have eaten all these dates of mine, it would be a long life". (The narrator said): He threw away all the dates he had with him. Then he fought the enemies until he was killed.

- 'Umair ibn Abd Amr ibn Nadlah

He was killed in Badr while he was about 30 years old

- 'Umair ibn Abu Waqas, brother of Saad

His mother was Hamna bint Abu Sufyan ibn Ummayyah. He was 16 years old at the time of battle of Badr. The Prophet (PBUH) refused his getting out to Badr but he wept, then the Prophet (PBUH) agreed. He was killed on the day of Badr by Amr ibn Abd Wud while he was 16 years old.

- 'Awf ibn 'Afraahe
- Mo'awz ibn 'Afra'
- Yazid ibn Alharith ibn Qais ibn Malik

Senior disbelievers died in this year

- Umayya ibn Abu Assalt

He was one of the atheists who did not believe in the Prophet despite he was aware that there would be a prophet; he was following the religion of Abraham. He lived during the prophethood of the Prophet and he met with him (PBUH). Some said that his pride and envy prevented him to convert to Islam. He was a great poet.

- Mut'im ibn ’Adi ibn Nawfal ibn Abd Manaf, Abu Wahb

He was one of Quraysh noble men. He was the man who protected the prophet when he returned from Ta'if. He died in Mecca when he was about 90 years old.

Jubair ibn Mut'im (May God be pleased with him) narrated, ‘The Messenger of God (PBUH) said concerning the prisoners of war taken at Badr, “If Almut'am ibn ’Adi had been alive and spoken to me about those filthy ones (as they were polytheists), I would have freed them for him. Related by Al-Bukhari.

- Abu Ahiha Said ibn Al'as ibn Ummayyah

He died in Ta'f when he was 90 years old. He was a great noble man in Mecca.

Then, 3rd Hijri year

Battle of Qarqaret Alkedr

It occurred in 15 Muharam where the Prophet (PBUH) went out to Alkedr (well for Banu Sulaym). The banner was held by Ali ibn Abu Talib (May God be pleased with him). Ibn Umm Maktoum was in charge of Medina. He knew that Banu Sulaym and Ghatfan were gathered there but when he reached this place, he found nothing but a boy who was grazing livestock. He took 500 camels as booty and returned to Medina.

Invasion of Sawiq

The Invasion of Sawiq occurred after the Quraysh's defeat in the Battle of Badr. After suffering the ignominious defeat at the Battle of Badr, Abu Sufyan ibn Harb, Quraysh leader, vowed that he would not bathe until he avenges his defeat. Abu Sufyan gathered two hundred men, took the eastern road through Nejd and secretly arrived by night, at the settlement of Banu Nadir, a Jewish tribe. Abu Sufyan took his men to the Urayd corn fields, a place about two or three miles to the north-east of Medina. He burnt these farms and killed 2 Muslims. Abu Sufyan and his men ran away. When Muhammad (PBUH) found out, he gathered his men, 200 men, and went behind Abu Sufyan. Abu Sufyan and his men, however, managed to flee. The Muslims managed to capture some of the sawiq (a type of flour) thrown away by Quraysh men, who did so to lighten their burden and flee.

Raid on Dhu Amarr (Ghatafan)

The raid on Amarr is also known as the Raid on Ghatafan that occurred directly after the Invasion of Sawiq in the 3rd Hijri year. The expedition was ordered by Muhammad after he received that Banu Muharib and Banu Tha'labah tribes were planning to raid the outskirts of Medina. When the enemies heard of the looming arrival of Muhammad, they quickly fled.

Jabur reported: We went forward with the Messenger of God (PBUH) and when we reached Dhat Arriqa', we came to a shady tree which -we left for him. One of the polytheists came there, seeing the sword of the Messenger (PBUH) hanging. He took it up and drew it from the scabbard and said to the Messenger of God (PBUH): Are you afraid of me? He (the Holy Prophet) said: No. He again said: Who would protect you from me? He said: God will protect me from you. The Companions of the Messenger of God (PBUH) threatened him. He sheathed the sword and hung it up.

Brigade of Kaab ibn Alashraf

Jabur reported: The Messenger of God (PBUH) said: Who will pursue Kaab ibn Alashraf, for he has caused trouble to God and His Prophet? Muhammad ibn Maslamah stood up and said: I (shall do), Messenger of God. Do you want that I should kill him? He said: Yes. He said: So permit me to say something (against you). He said: Yes say. He then came to him (Kaab ibn Alashraf) and said to him: This man has asked us for sadaqah (alms) and has put us into trouble. Kaab said: You will be more grieved. Muhammad ibn Maslamah said: We have followed him and we do not like to forsake him until we see what will be the consequences of his matter. We wished if you could lend us one or two wasqs. Kaab said: What will you mortgage with me? He asked: what do you want from us? He replied: Your women. They said: Glory be to God: You are the most beautiful of the Arabs. If we mortgage our women with you, that will be a disgrace for us. He said “Then mortgage your children.” He replied: “No, we shall mortgage a coat of mail with you. By this he meant arms”. He said “Yes, when he came to him, he called him and he came out while he used perfume and his head was spreading fragrance. When he met with him and he came there accompanied by three or four persons who mentioned his perfume. He said “I have such and such woman with me. She is the most fragrant of the women among the people. He (Muhammed ibn Maslamah) asked “Do you permit me so that I may smell? He said “Yes. He then entered his hand through his hair and smells it.” He said “May I repeat?” He said “Yes.” He again entered his hand through his hair. When he got his complete control, he struck him until death.”

Marriage of Uthman ibn Affan to Umm Kulthum

In this year, Uthman ibn Affan married to Umm Kulthum.

Invasion of Banu Sulaym

In this year, the prophet (PBUH) went out to Banu Sulaym on 6th of Jumada I. He knew that there a gathering at Banu Sulaym, so he went out together with 300 men but when he reached them, he found them departed.

Brigade of Zaid ibn Harithah (Alqarada raid)

Alqarada raid took place in Jumada II. It was the first brigade headed by Zaid ibn Harithah. Alqarada was the name of a well. The Prophet sent him together with 100 riders to intercept a caravan of Quraysh. They successfully raided it and captured 100,000 dirhams worth of booty.

His marriage (PBUH) to Hafsah

She was married to Khunais ibn Hudhaifah but became a widow. As soon as Hafsah had completed her widow period, her father Umar offered her hand to Uthman Ibn 'Affan, and thereafter to Abu Bakr; but they both refused her. When Umar went to Muhammad to complain about this, Muhammad replied, "God will marry Uthman to better than your daughter and will marry your daughter to better than Uthman."

Muhammad (PBUH) married to Hafsah in Sha'ban in the 3rd Hijri year. This marriage gave the Prophet the chance of allying himself with this faithful follower, Umar, who then became his father-in-law.

His marriage (PBUH) to Zaynab bint Khuzayma

She was also known as Umm Almasakin, "Mother of the Poor". Zaynab was first married to Tufail ibn Harith, who either divorced her or died shortly afterward. Zaynab then married her first husband's brother, Ubaydah ibn Alharith. Her husband died of wounds received in the Battle of Badr. The Prophet (PBUH) married to her in Ramadan in that year.

Also, in this year, Hassan ibn Ali, May God be pleased with them; is said to be born in Ramadan.

Battle of Uhud

It is one of the events that occurred in this year. It occurred on Saturday 7th of Shawwal at the valley located in front of Mount Uhud. A number of the leading tribesmen of Quraysh had been killed at Badr and so leadership passed to Abu Sufyan. He forbade the mourning of the losses at Badr, for he was eager to take revenge from Muhammad, vowing to conduct a punitive raid on Medina. Quraysh noble men went to Abu Sufyan offering him their caravan to sell it and prepare an army to take revenge from the Prophet (PBUH) and his companions. Abu Sufyan invited all Arab tribes to fight with him; he raised another force numbering 3,000 and set out for the Muslim base in Medina.

A scout ('Abbas ibn Abdulmutalib) alerted Muhammad of the Meccan army's presence and size. On the following morning, a Muslim conference of war was held, and there was dispute over how to best repel the Meccans. Muhammad and many of the senior figures suggested that it would be sounder to fight within Medina and make use of its heavily armored strongholds. Younger Muslims argued that the Meccans were destroying their crops, and that nestling in the strongholds would destroy Muslim stature. Muhammad in the long run accepted this opinion, and prepared the Muslim force for battle.

The Prophet made three banners; the banner of Al'aws was handed to Usaid ibn Hudair, banner of Khazraj was handed to Alhabab and that of Almuhajirun was handed to Ali. Abdullah ibn Umm Maktoum assumed the charge of Medina.

Approximately 1,000 Muslim men set out on late Friday from Medina and managed to siege the Meccan forces. Early on the following morning, they took a position on the lower slopes of the hill of Uhud. Right Away before the battle started, 'Abdullah ibn Ubayy (the chief of the Khazraj tribe) and his followers retracted from their support for Muhammad and returned to Medina.

The Muslim force, became around 700, it was situated on the slopes of Uhud, being guarded by the towering mount itself.

Before the battle, Muhammad had assigned 50 archers on a neighboring rocky hill at the west side of the Muslim camp site. This was a strategic decision in order to protect the defenseless flanks of the outnumbered Muslim army; the archers on the hill were to guard the left flank, whereas the right flank was protected by the Mount of Uhud located on the east side of the Muslim camp.

The Meccan army positioned itself facing the Muslim forces, led by Abu Sufyan, and the left and right flanks commanded by Ikrimah ibn Abu Jahl and Khalid ibn Alwalid respectively. 'Amr ibn Al'as was named the commander of cavalry and his task was to coordinate attack between the cavalry wings.

The Meccan banner was held by Talhah ibn Abu Talhah Alabdari, who advanced and challenged the enemy to a battle. Ali ibn Abu Talib, the young cousin of Muhammad, rushed forth and struck Talhah down in a single blow. Yet, Uthman, Talhah's brother progressed to pick up the fallen banner. Hamza ibn Abdulmutalib came to kill Uthman. It was their family that was accountable for the Meccan army's banner, and thus one by one, Talhah's brothers and sons went to rescue the Meccan banner and fight in vain, until they all finally met their end. Following the battle, general conflict between the two armies began.

The Meccan army was pushed back, and frequent attempts by its cavalry to invade the left Muslim flank were contradicted by the Muslim archers. The Muslims pierced through the Meccan lines, with victory appearing sure. Though, it was the detachment of the Muslim archers who violating Muhammad's strict orders to remain at their place as they ran downhill to join in the advance and ruin the Meccan camp, leaving the flank at risk.

At this critical moment, the Meccan cavalry led by Khalid ibn Alwalid made use of this move and attacked the outstanding minority of Muslim archers who refused to violate Muhammad's orders and were still located on the hill. Thus, Meccans were then able to attack the Muslim flank and rear, as a result, numerous Muslims lives were claimed.

While the Meccan riposte strengthened, rumors went viral that Muhammad too died. Muhammad had only been wounded, due to missiles of stone which resulted in a wound on his forehead. It is said that Ali ibn Abu Talib alone remained, fending off the attacks of Khalid's forces.

Hamza who had been thrown down in by an arrow of the Abyssinian slave of Hind, Wahshi ibn Harib.

Al bara' ibn Azib said "On the day of the battle of Uhud, the Prophet (PBUH) appointed `Abdullah ibn Jubair as the commander of the infantry men (archers) who were fifty on the day (of the battle) of Uhud. He instructed them, to stick to their places, till further instructions; and if they see that they have defeated the infidels, even then they should not leave their place till further instructions." Then the infidels were defeated. "By God, I saw the women fleeing lifting up their clothes revealing their leg-bangles and their legs. So, the companions of `Abdullah ibn Jubair said, "The booty! O people, the booty! Your companions have become victorious, what are you waiting for now?" `Abdullah ibn Jubair said, "Have you forgotten what God's Messenger (PBUH) said to you?" They replied, "By God! We will go to the people (i.e. the enemy) and collect our share from the war booty." But when they went to them, they were forced to turn back beaten. At that time God's Messenger (PBUH) in their rear was calling them back. Only twelve men remained with the Prophet (PBUH) and the infidels martyred seventy men from us."

On the day of the battle of Badr, the Prophet (PBUH) and his companions had caused the infidels to lose 140 men, seventy of whom were captured and seventy were killed. Abu Sufyan asked thrice, "Is Muhammad present amongst these people?" The Prophet (PBUH) ordered his companions not to answer him. Then he asked thrice, "Is ibn Abu Quhafa present amongst these people?" He asked again thrice, "Is ibn Alkhattab present amongst these people?" He then returned to his companions and said, "As for these (men), they have been killed." `Umar could not control himself and said to Abu Sufyan, "You are telling a lie, by God! O' enemy of God! All those you have mentioned are alive, and the thing which will make you disappointed is still there." Abu Sufyan said, "Our victory today is an offset to yours in the battle of Badr, and in war, the victory is always unresolved and is shared in turns by the belligerents, and you will find some of your killed men mutilated, but I did not urge my men to do so, yet I do not feel sorry for their deed" Then he started declaiming joyfully, "O Hubal, be high!"

Accordingly, the Prophet (PBUH) said to his companions, "Why don't you answer him back?" They said, "O God's Messenger (PBUH), what shall we say?" He said, "Say, God is Higher and more Sublime." Abu Sufyan said, "We have the Al `Uzza, and you have no `Uzza." The Prophet said to his companions, "Why don't you answer him back?" They asked, "O God's Messenger (PBUH), what shall we say?" He said, "God is our Helper and you have no helper."

Hind and her companions are said to have mutilated the Muslim corpses, cutting their ears and noses and making the relics into anklets. Hind is reported to have open the corpse of Hamza, taking out his liver which she attempted to eat.

Abu Sufyan, after some conversations with Muhammad's companion, Umar ibn Alkhattab, decided to go back to Mecca without using the full potential.

The Prophet (PBUH) told Ali to tail the people to check if they rode camels or horses. Ali followed them and found them rode camels returning to mecca.

Ubayy ibn Kaab narrated: "On the Day of Uhud, sixty-four of Ansar were killed, and six from AlMuhajirin, one of whom was Hamzah, and they mutilated them, so Ansar said: 'If, (in the future) we are able to kill them on a day like this, we would mutilate from among them as twice as they (mutilate from among us).'" He said: "So on the day of the Conquest of Mecca, God has revealed: " And if you punish [an enemy, O believers], punish with an equivalent of that with which you were harmed. But if you are patient - it is better for those who are patient"." وَإِنْ عَاقَبْتُمْ فَعَاقِبُوا بِمِثْلِ مَا عُوقِبْتُم بِهِ، وَلَئِن صَبَرْتُمْ لَهُوَ خَيْرٌ لِّلصَّابِرِينَ" (16:126). So a man said: 'There shall be no Quraysh after today."

Hamza ibn Abdulmutalib was killed by Wahshi. There were 70 men killed from Ansar while there were 23 men killed from Quraysh.

The Prophet (PBUH) ordered Muslims to bury their dead men saying: "Dig deep and bury those who maintain Quran at first."

The Prophet commended Muslims to bury their dead men in their places of killing.

Then the Prophet went back to Medina, Hammanah bint Jahsh met the Prophet (PBUH) who said: "O Hammanah! Expect that your brother Abdullah will be rewarded!" She replied, "To God we belong and to him we shall return. May God's mercy be upon him and may God forgive him." Then Muhammad said, "Expect that your maternal uncle, Hamza ibn Abdulmutalib, will be rewarded!" Again she remained calm and gave the same reply. He then said, "O Hammanah! Expect that your husband, Musaab ibn `Umair, will be rewarded!" Upon this she cried and wailed. Muhammad remarked, "The woman's husband holds a special place with her, as you can see from her self-control at the death of her brother and her uncle and her screaming over her husband."

On the day of Uhud, people of Medina were screaming as it was said to them that Muhammad (PBUH) was killed. A woman from Khazraj went to the outskirts of Medina, she received her brother, father, husband and son killed but she asked about the Prophet (PBUH), then she went to him saying: "May my mother and father be sacrificed for you!"

Battle of Hamra' Alasad

On Sunday the 8th of Shawaal, the day after the battle of Uhud, when the Muslims woke up, they heard that Muhammad (PBUH) had called on them to join him in the pursuit of the returning Quraysh army. He gave a general order of mobilization, with the condition that only those who had participated in Uhud battle were worthy to participate in the new one. One Muslim, who missed the battle of Uhud as his father did not allow him to fight at Uhud, was agreed to join the Muslim army. The son of a martyred soldier requested Muhammad's permission to join this expedition and was also allowed to participate. Several wounded fighters also joined the march. The Prophet went out till he reached Hamra' Alasad. He gave Ali the banner which was still held. The Prophet left the charge of Medina to Abdullah ibn Maktoum.

Shortly before Muhammad set out tracking the returning Meccan army, he sent three spies, all belonging to Banu Aslam, to tail the departing Meccan army. Two of them met the Meccan army at Hamra Alasad, eight miles from Medina. Abu Sufyan had heard about Muhammad's endeavor to follow the Meccans. The two spies heard the discussion among Quraysh: whether they should go back and beat the Muslims or to continue their journey to Mecca.

This happened a day before the Meccans reached Hamra Alasad. Prior to their departure from Hamra Alasad, Quraysh found the two Muslim spies, then killed them, leaving their corpses on the road. The third Muslim spy's location was not known.

The Muslim fighters, led by Muhammad, went to Hamra Alasad and found the two dead bodies of their spies. Once Muhammad learned that Quraysh were not there to attack him further, he chose to spend three nights before returning to Medina.

Abu Azzah Aljumahi was seized as a captive. Abu Azzah had previously been one of the captives of Badr. Abu Azzah Amr ibn Abd Allah Aljumahi had been well-treated by Muhammad after the Battle of Badr, being a poor man having daughters, he had no means to pay ransom, he was released after Battle of Badr, provided that he would not fight against Muslims again. But he had not fulfilled his promise and participated in Battle of Uhud. He was an influential poet who exploited his poetry to mobilize the masses against Muhammad. During the Battle of Uhud, he used his poetry again to mobilize the masses against Muhammad. He also joined other Arab infidels to the Battle of Uhud. He was captured again and stated "O Muhammad let me free, I was forced to come". He begged for mercy again, but Muhammad ordered him to be killed. Azzubayr executed him, and in another version, Asim ibn Thabit.

Tale of those who were killed in this year

- Anas ibn Nadhar ibn Dhamdham ibn Zaid ibn Haram

He belonged to the Banu Khazraj tribe of Ansar and was the uncle of Anas ibn Malik. He could not join the Battle of Badr and was sad about it.

He fought against the polytheists in the Battle of Uhud until he was martyred.

Anas ibn Malik narrated: "My paternal uncle Anas ibn Nadhar - after whom I was named - did not participate in the battle of

Badr with the Messenger of God (PBUH). This distressed him and he said: 'I was absent from the first battle which the Messenger of God (PBUH) attended. By God! If God gives me the opportunity to participate in another battle along with the Messenger of God (PBUH), then God will see what I will do!'" He said: "He did not want to say more than that. A year later, he attended the battle of Uhud, where he saw Saad ibn Mu'adh and said: 'O Abu 'Amr where are you going?' He said: 'I long for the fragrance of Paradise and I have found it near the mountains of Uhud.' He fought them until he was killed. They found more than eighty wounds on his body. My paternal aunt was who could recognize him except by his fingertips.' And this verse was revealed: "Among the believers are men true to what they promised God. Among them is he who has fulfilled his vow [to the death], and among them is he who awaits [his chance]. And they did not alter [the terms of their commitment] by any alteration"." مِّنَ الْمُؤْمِنِينَ رِجَالٌ صَدَقُوا مَا عَاهَدُوا اللَّهَ عَلَيْهِ، فَمِنْهُم مَّن قَضَىٰ نَحْبَهُ وَمِنْهُم مَّن يَنتَظِرُ، وَمَا بَدَّلُوا تَبْدِيلًا" (33:23)."

- 'Unais ibn Qatadah ibn Rabi'ah

He fought in Badr and Uhud and he was killed in Uhud.

- Thabit ibn Adahdah

He was one of Muslims who stand fighting infidels despite he heard that the Prophet was killed. He stood and said if

Muhammad was killed, then, fight for the God of Muhammad but he was killed by a spear of Khalid ibn Alwalid.

Some scholars said that his wounds were cured and he died while the Prophet (PBUH) was returning from Treaty of Hudaybiyyah.

- Thabit ibn Amr ibn Zaid ibn 'Adi

He fought in Badr and Uhud but he was killed in Uhud.

- Janda' ibn Dhara Aldhamari

He was ill in Mecca. He asked his sons to get him out to Medina; migrate to Medina. While they were in their way to Medina, he died. God has revealed: "And whoever leaves his home as an emigrant to God and His Messenger and then death overtakes him - his reward has already become incumbent upon God. And God is ever Forgiving and Merciful"." وَمَن يَخْرُجْ مِن بَيْتِهِ مُهَاجِرًا إِلَى اللَّـهِ وَرَسُولِهِ ثُمَّ يُدْرِكْهُ الْمَوْتُ فَقَدْ وَقَعَ أَجْرُهُ عَلَى اللَّـهِ ، وَكَانَ اللَّـهُ غَفُورًا رَّحِيمًا" (4:100).

- Alharith ibn 'Aws ibn Mu'az ibn Annu'man

He fought in Badr and he killed Kaab ibn Alashraf. He fought at Uhud and he was killed when he was 28 years.

- Hamza ibn Abdulmuttalib ibn Hashim ibn Abd Manaf

His mother is Halah bint Uhayb ibn Abd Manaf ibn Zuhrah. The first banner to be held was by Hamza. The Prophet (PBUH) set fraternal bond between him and Zaid ibn Harithah. He was killed in the battle of Uhud by the Abyssinian slave Wahshi ibn

Harb. Wahshi then slit open his stomach and brought his liver to Hind bint Utbah, whose father Hamza had killed at Badr. Hind chewed Hamza's liver then spat it out.

Jafar ibn `Amr ibn Umaiya narrated: "I went out with 'Ubaidullah ibn `Adi Alkhaiyar. When we reached Hims (i.e. a town in Syria), 'Ubaidullah ibn `Adi said (to me), "Would you like to see Wahshi so that we may ask him about the killing of Hamza?" I replied, "Yes." Wahshi used to live in Hims. We enquired about him and somebody said to us, "He is that in the shade of his palace, as if he were a full water skin." So we went up to him, and when we were at a short distance from him, we greeted him and he greeted us in return. 'Ubaidullah was wearing his turban and Wahshi could not see except his eyes and feet. 'Ubaidullah said, "O Wahshi! Do you know me?" Wahshi looked at him and then said, "No, by God! But I know that `Adi ibn Alkhiyar married a woman called Um Qital, the daughter of Abu Al-Is, and she delivered a boy for him at Mecca, and I looked for a wet nurse for that child. (Once) I carried that child along with his mother and then I handed him over to her, and your feet resemble that child's feet." Then 'Ubaidullah uncovered his face and said (to Wahshi), "Will you tell us (the story of) the killing of Hamza?" Wahshi replied "Yes, Hamza killed Tuaima ibn `Adi ibn Al-Khaiyar at Badr (battle) so my master, Jubair ibn Mut`im said to me, 'If you kill Hamza in revenge for my uncle, then you will be set free." When the people set out (for the battle of Uhud) in the year of 'Ainain. 'Ainain is a mountain near the mountain of Uhud, and between it and Uhud there is a valley. I went out with the people for the battle. When the army aligned for the fight, Siba' came out and said, 'Is there any (Muslim) to accept my challenge to a duel?' Hamza ibn `Abdulmuttalib came out and said, 'O Siba'. O Ibn Um Anmar, the one who circumcises other ladies! Do you challenge God and His Apostle?' Then Hamza attacked and killed him, causing him to be non-extant like the bygone yesterday. I hid myself under a rock, and when he (i.e. Hamza) came near me, I threw my spear at him, driving it into his umbilicus so that it came out through his buttocks, causing him to die. When all the people returned to Mecca, I too returned with them. I stayed in (Mecca) till Islam spread in it (i.e. Mecca). Then I left for Ta'if, and when the people (of Ta'if) sent their messengers to God's Messenger (PBUH), I was told that the Prophet (PBUH) did not harm the messengers; So I too went out with them till I reached God's Messenger (PBUH). When he saw me, he said, 'Are you Wahshi?' I said, 'Yes.' He said, 'Was it you who killed Hamza?' I replied, 'What happened is what you have been told of.' He said, 'Can you hide your face from me?' So I went out when God's Messenger (PBUH) died, and Musailamah Alkadhdhab appeared (claiming to be a prophet). I said, 'I will go out to Musailamah so that I may kill him, and make amends for killing

Hamza. So I went out with the people (to fight Musailamah and his followers) and then famous events took place concerning that battle. Suddenly I saw a man (i.e. Musailamah) standing near a gap in a wall. He looked like an ash-colored camel and his hair was disheveled. So I threw my spear at him, driving it into his chest in between his breasts till it passed out through his shoulders, and then an Ansari man attacked him and struck him on the head with a sword. `Abdullah ibn `Umar said, 'A slave girl on the roof of a house said: Alas! The chief of the believers (i.e. Musailamah) has been killed by a black slave."

- Hanzalah ibn Abu 'Amir

Hanzala ibn Abu 'Amir was one of the companions of Prophet Muhammad. He belonged to Banu 'Aws tribe of Ansar. His father, Abu 'Amir was Christian. Hanzala's was just 24 years when he was killed in the Battle of Uhud while fighting against the polytheists. He was an infantry, he attacked Abu Sufyan ibn Harb. However, the latter was rescued by Shaddad ibn Alaswad who also killed Hanzala.

Hanzala had earlier gone for the battlefield to respond the call of Jihad leaving his wife Jamila, sister of Abdullah ibn Ubayy, on the first night after wedding. He did not have the time for doing ablution. Muhammad is narrated to have seen angels giving Hanzala a bath in between heavens and the earth with fresh rainwater kept in silver bowls. Hanzala earned the title of Ghaseel Almalāʾika (one cleansed by the angels).

- Kharjah ibn Zayd ibn Abu Zuhair

Kharjah ibn Zayd is the father of Zaid, who spoke after his death. He witnessed the second Aqaba pledge and the Battle of Badr and he was killed in the Battle of Uhud.

Prophet Muhammad (PBUH) set the bond of fraternity between him and Abu Bakr, who married his daughter Habiba, and gave birth to Umm Kulthum.

- Khunais ibn Hudhaifa ibn Qais ibn 'Adi ibn Saad

Khunais ibn Hudhaifa converted to Islam before the Prophet entered Dar ibn Alarqam. He joined the migration to Abyssinia. He married Hafsa bint Umar. Khunais was the only member of the Sahm clan who fought at the Battle of Badr. He was buried at Albaqi' beside the grave of Uthman ibn Maz'un.

- Khaythmah ibn Alharith ibn Malik ibn Kaab

He was the father of Saad ibn Khaythmah. He went out with the Prophet to Uhud where he was killed there.

- Zkawan bin Abdul Qais ibn Khaldah

Zkawan went to Mecca together with Asaad ibn Zerara. They met Prophet Muhammad (PBUH) and they listened to his speech, then they converted to Islam and returned to Yathrib (Medina); He was the first from Ansar to convert into Islam. Zkwan fought in the Battle of Badr. He was killed by Abu Alhakam ibn Alakhnis who was killed by Ali.

- Rafi' ibn Malik ibn Al'ajlan

It is said that he together with Mu'az ibn Al'afra' are the first Ansari to convert to Islam when they met the Prophet (PBUH) in Mecca. He attended Aqaba II together with 70 men; he was one of the twelve leaders. He did not fight at Badr but he fought at Uhud and he was killed then.

- Rafi' ibn Yazid ibn Karz

He fought at Badr and Uhud and he was killed then.

- Saad ibn Arrabi' ibn Amr ibn Abu Zuhair

He was one of the 12th leaders who attended the Aqaba Pledge of Allegiance. He fought at Badr and Uhud, he was martyred in the battle of Uhud.

- Shammas ibn 'Uthman ibn Alsharid

Shammas ibn Uthman fought at Badr and Uhud. The Messenger of God (PBUH) did not throw his eyes to the right or to the left unless he saw Shamas in that turn fighting using his sword until he was killed protecting the Prophet (PBUH) at Uhud while Muslims fled and left the Prophet (PBUH). He was brought to Medina.

The Messenger of God (PBUH) said: "Take him to Umm Salamah" and he was carried to her and he died. Then the Messenger of God (PBUH) ordered him to be taken back to Uhud where he was buried there as he was in his clothes. He died when he was thirty-four years old. May God have mercy on him

- Abdullah ibn Jubair ibn Alnu'manibn Ummayyah

He attended Aqaba pledge with the seventy men. He fought at Badr and Uhud. The Prophet (PBUH) appointed him then on the head of the archers. When the archers left Uhud to gather the bouty, he stayed together with 10 archers till his arrows finished and he was killed by 'Ikremah ibn Abu Jahl.

- Abdullah ibn Jahsh ibn Reyab ibn Ya'mur ibn Sabra

He was son of Umama bint Abdulmuttalib, he converted to Islam before the Prophet (PBUH) entered the house of Arqam. The Prophet (PBUH) sent him to Nakhla and he was handed the first banner to be held by the Prophet (PBUH).

- Abdullah ibn Amr ibn Huzam, Abu Jabir:

He witnessed Aqaba pledge with the seventy men. He fought at Badr and Uhud. He was killed then.

Jabir ibn `Abdullah narrated: God's Messenger (PBUH) used to veil two martyrs of Uhud in one sheet and then say, "Which of them knew Qur'an more?" When one of the two was pointed out, he would put him first in the grave. Then he said, "I will be a witness for them on the Day of Resurrection." He ordered them to be buried with their blood (on their bodies). No funeral prayer was offered to any of them, nor they washed. Jabir added, "When my father was martyred, I started weeping and uncovering his face. The companions of the Prophet (PBUH) stopped me from doing so but the Prophet (PBUH) did not stop me. Then the Prophet said, '(O Jabir.) don't weep over him, for the angels kept on covering him with their wings till his body was carried away (for burial)."

- Amr ibn Thabit ibn Waqsh ibn Zughbah

His mother is Layla, the sister of Hudhaifa ibn Alyaman. He was converted to Islam while the Prophet was at Uhud, he fought at Uhud till he was killed. When he was asked why he was at Uhud, he said for 'Islam'.

- Uthman ibn Maz'oon

He abandoned alcohol before Islam era. He had converted to Islam before the Prophet (PBUH) entered to the house of Alarqam.

He led a group of Muslims to Abyssinia in the first migration which some of the early Muslims undertook to escape persecution in Mecca.

He fought at Badr and he died in the 3rd year after the Hijrah and was either the first companion or the first Muhajir to be buried in the cemetery of Baqi' in Medina.

- Amr ibn Aljamuh ibn Zaid ibn Haram:

He was disabled and he did not fight at Badr but he fought at Uhud. He was killed together with his son Khalad at Uhud.

- Malik ibn Sinan ibn Thaalabah ibn 'Ubaid ibn Alabhar, the father of Abu Said Alkhudri

He fought at Uhud and he was killed by Gharab ibn Sufyan.

- Musaab ibn 'Umair ibn Hashim ibn Abd Manaf ibn Abd Aldar ibn Qusai:

He married to Hammanah bint Jahsh. He was a very handsome young man, his parents were very rich.

The first Muslims used to meet with Muhammad at the house of Alarqam known as the islamic learning center. Musaab went to this house to find out more about Islam. As a result of hearing the reciting of the Qur'an and the preaching of Muhammad, he converted. At first Musaab kept his faith a secret but only for one day, Uthman ibn Talha, saw him entering Alarqam house and joining the Muslim prayers. The news went viral and eventually reached his mother, who chained him in their house with the intention of making him renounce this belief. Musaab would not renounce his faith. Muhammad advised him to join the companions who were migrating to Abyssinia so that he would not be harassed again.

Musaab ibn Umayr was appointed the first ambassador of Islam and was sent to Yathrib (Medina) to prepare the city for the forthcoming Hijra after the first pledge with Ansar. A man of Medina named Saad ibn Zurarah assisted him. After they had called for Islam, many residents of Medina converted, including such leading men such as Saad ibn Muadh, Usayd ibn Hudayr and Saad ibn Ubadah.

Musaab ibn 'Umair went out together with the seventy men from Medina to Mecca, who went to swore pledge to the Prophet (PBUH).

The banner of Almuhajirun was held by him at Badr and Uhud. During the battle of Uhud, some Muslims were under the impression that the war was over, they left their positions on the battlefield, giving the opposing forces hope of attacking the Prophet (PBUH), he raised his voice saying 'God is the greatest' to attract the attention of disbelievers so that they did not attack the Prophet (PBUH) and he could escape unhurt. Musaab was attacked, and his right hand was severed holding the Flag, but he continued to repeat the Quranic words: "Muhammad is not but a messenger. [Other] messengers have passed on before him"." وَمَا مُحَمَّدٌ إِلَّا رَسُولٌ قَدْ خَلَتْ مِن قَبْلِهِ الرُّسُلُ" (3:144), and took the flag in his left hand. When his left hand was severed he took hold of it with his arms but never let the flag fall and he continued to repeat the Quranic words: "Muhammad is not but a messenger. [Other] messengers have passed on before him"." وَمَا مُحَمَّدٌ إِلَّا رَسُولٌ قَدْ خَلَتْ مِن قَبْلِهِ الرُّسُلُ" (3:144). Eventually Musab was hit by a spear thrown by Ibn Kami'ah and died. But never let the flag fall while he had breath in his chest.

The Prophet (PBUH) stood before Musaab ibn 'Umair and said: "Among the believers are men true to what they promised God. Among them is he who has fulfilled his vow [to the death], and among them is he who awaits [his chance]. And they did not alter [the terms of their commitment] by any alteration"." مِّنَ الْمُؤْمِنِينَ رِجَالٌ صَدَقُوا مَا عَاهَدُوا اللَّـهَ عَلَيْهِ، فَمِنْهُم مَّن قَضَىٰ نَحْبَهُ وَمِنْهُم مَّن يَنتَظِرُ، وَمَا بَدَّلُوا تَبْدِيلً" (33:23). He died while he was 42 years old.

Khabbab Alaratt reported: 'We migrated with the Messenger of God (PBUH) in the path of God seeking God's pleasure alone. Thus our reward was assured with God. And amongst us were those who spent life (in such a state of piety and austerity) that nothing consumed their reward. Musaab ibn 'Umair was one of them. He was killed on the Day of Uhud, and nothing but a woollen cloak was found to shroud him. When we covered his head with it, his feet became uncovered, and when we covered his feet, his head was uncovered. Upon this the Messenger of God (PBUH) said: Place it (this cloak) on the side of his head and cover his feet with grass. And there is one amongst us for whom the fruit is ripened and he enjoys it.'

- Wahhab ibn Qaboos Almuzni

It is narrated that Wahhab ibn Qaboos Almuzni, along with his nephew Alharith ibn 'Uqbah ibn Qaboos, came to them with sheep from the mountain of Muzina, they found the city empty. They asked: 'Where the people?', they were told them that Muslims were fighting Quraysh at Mount Uhud. They converted to Islam, then, they went out to the Prophet (PBUH) and found that Muslims were looting. Then, a group of the Quraysh was divided, and the Prophet (PBUH) said: "Who will stop this group?" Wahab ibn Qaboos said: "I will, Messenger of God." So he shot them with arrows until they left. Then another group came, and the Prophet Muhammad said, "Who will stop this group?" Wahhab said, "I will, Messenger of God." So he fought them with the sword until they went. Then, he returned. Then, there was another group, and the Prophet said: "Who will stop these men?" He said, "I am, Messenger of God." The Prophet (PBUH) said, "stand up and you will enter the Heaven." So the Muzni said, "O God, I do not dismiss or resign." Then, he died and the Prophet (PBUH) said: "Oh God, have mercy on him." His nephew Alharith ibn 'Uqba, who fought like his uncle until he was killed. The Prophet (PBUH): "May God be pleased with you. I am satisfied with you."

Fourth Hijri year

Some events:

Expedition of Qatan (Detachment of Abu Salamah ibn Abd Alasad)

It was in Muhharram after after the Battle of Hamra Alasad in the 4th Hijri year. The Prophet (PBUH), after he received intelligence that some members of the Banu Asad ibn Khuzaymah were planning to attack Medina, dispatched Abu Salama together with 150 men holding a banner to make a sudden attack on this tribe.

When the Muslims arrived at the site, the tribe members fled and the Muslims found three herdsmen with a large herd of camels and goats. Then the booty, along with the three captives, was brought to Medina.

Expedition of Abdullah Ibn Unais

The Expedition of Abdullah ibn Unais, also known as the Assassination of Sufyan ibn Khalid, it was the 1st attack against the Banu Lahyan, which took place in the month of Muhharram in the 4th Hijri year.

It was reported that Sufyan ibn Khalid Alhathali (also known as Hudayr, the chief of the Banu Lahyan tribe), considered an attack on Medina and that he was inciting the people on Nakhla or Uranah to fight Muslims. So The Prophet (PBUH) sent Abdullah ibn Unais to assassinate him. Abdullah ibn Unais found Hudayr in the company of his wife, when asked about his identity. Unais replied: "I am an arab tribesman who has heard of you and the Army you are raising to fight The Prophet (PBUH), so I have come to join your ranks"

Sufyan ibn Khalid trusted him. Then Unais asked to talk to him privately, once, while conversing, Abdullah ibn Unais walked a short distance with ibn Khalid, and when an opportunity came he struck him with his sword and killed him. After killing ibn Khalid, he cut off his head, brought that to the Prophet (PBUH). The Prophet (PBUH) gave him his staff as a reward and said: "This will function as a sign of recognition for you and me, on the day of resurrection".

Detachment of Almundhir ibn Amr AlSaadi to the Well of Ma'una

It occurred in Safar. It happened that Amer ibn Malik came to the Prophet (PBUH) and the Prophet invited to Islam but he did not convert to Islam. He said if you sent some men from your companions, His people would accept the call for Islam.

Anas narrated: "The Prophet (PBUH) sent seventy men from the tribe of Banu Salim to the tribe of Banu Amir. When they reached there, my maternal uncle said to them, "I will go ahead of you, and if they allow me to convey the message of The Prophet (PBUH) (it will be all right); otherwise you will remain close to me." So he went ahead of them and the pagans granted him security but while he was reporting the message of the Prophet (PBUH) , they beckoned to one of their men who stabbed him to death. My maternal uncle said, "God is Greater! By the Lord of the Kaaba, I am successful." After that they attached the rest of the party and killed them all except a lame man who went up to the top of the mountain. (Hammam, a sub-narrator said, "I think another man was saved along with him)." Gabriel informed the Prophet (PBUH) that they (i.e the martyrs) met their Lord, and He was pleased with them and made them pleased. We used to recite, "Inform our people that we have met our Lord, He is pleased with us and He has made us pleased." Later on this Qur'anic Verse was cancelled. The Prophet (PBUH) invoked God for forty days to curse the murderers from the tribe of Ral, Dhakwan, Banu Lahyan and Bam Usaiya who disobeyed God and his Prophet (PBUH)."

Detachment of Marthad ibn Abu Marthad Alghanawi to Alraji'

It is said that some people went to the Prophet (PBUH) and said that there were muslims among them and they wanted some men to let them be aware to Islam. The Prophet (PBUH) sent ten men with them; the Prophet sent him to Mecca in the Alraji' Expedition, leading ten other friends. He was killed in an expedition that took place in Safar.

Abu Hurairah said “The Prophet (PBUH) sent ten persons (on an expedition) and appointed Asim ibn Thabut as their commander. About one hundred men of Hudhail who were archers came out to attack them. When ‘Asim felt their presence, they took cover in a hillock. They said to them “Come down and surrender and we will make a covenant and pact with you that we shall not kill any of you”. Asim said “I do not come to the protection of a disbeliever". Then they shot them with arrows and killed Asim in a company of seven persons. The other three persons came down to their covenant and pact. They were Khubaib, Zaid ibn Allathnah and another man. When they overpowered them, they untied their bow strings and tied them with them". The third person said "This is the first treachery. I swear by God, I shall not accompany you. In them (my companions) is an example for me." They pulled him, but he refused to accompany them, so they killed him. Khubaib remained their captive until they agreed to kill him. He asked for a razor to shave his pubes. When they brought him outside to kill him. Khubaib said to them "Let me offer two rak'ahs of prayer". He then said "I swear by God, if you did not think that I did this out of fear, I would have increased (the number of rak'ahs)."

Then, there was

Invasion of Banu Nadir in Rabi' I of the 4th Hijri year

The reason behind it is that the Prophet (PBUH) with some of his Companions set out to see the Banu Nadir tribe and seek their help in raising the blood-money he had to pay to the Banu Kilab for the two men that Amr ibn Omaiyah Addamari had killed by mistake in the Expedition of Bir Maona. On hearing his story, they said they would share the blood-money and asked him and his Companions Abu Bakr, Umar, Ali and others to sit under a wall of their houses and wait. Gabriel came down to reveal the plot by the Banu Nadir that was to murder The Prophet (PBUH), so he and his Companions, return to Medina. On their way, he told his Companions of the Divine Revelation. The Banu Nadir Jews held a brief meeting and they conspired to kill him.

The Prophet (PBUH) ordered them to leave Medina within ten days. The tribe at first decided to obey, but Abdullah ibn Ubayy, the chief of the Khazraj, persuaded them to resist in their fortresses, promising to send 2,000 men to their aid. Huyayy ibn Akhtab decided to stick to resistance, hoping for help from Banu Quraiza, despite having opposition within the tribe.

The Banu Nadir regained their confidence and were determined to fight. Their chief Huyai ibn Akhtab relied hopefully on what Abdullah ibn Ubayy promised. Thus, he sent a message to The Prophet (PBUH) saying: "We will not leave our houses. Do whatever you like."

Muslims made the decisions of taking up arms whatever the consequences could bring. When the The Prophet (PBUH) received the reply of Huyai ibn Akhtab he said: "God is the Greatest, God is the Greatest." and his Companions repeated after him. Then he left to fight them after appointing Ibn Umm Maktum to dispose the affairs of Medina during his absence. Banu Nadir resorted to their castles, mounted them and started shooting arrows and throwing stones towards the Muslims appreciating the advantage that their thick fields of palm trees provided. The

Muslims were therefore ordered to burn those trees. Quraiza tribe remained unbiased, and Abdullah ibn Ubayyas and Ghatafan failed to keep their promises of support to Banu Nadir.

In this year, Husayn ibn Ali (May God be pleased with them) was born on 3rd of Sha'aban.

Then, there was Expedition of Badr Almawid on 1st of Dhul Qidah

A year after the Battle of Uhud, it was time for Muslims to meet the polytheists and start war again in order to determine which of the two parties was worthy of survival.

The two opposing forces were to meet again at Badr, and that year there was a great drought, Abu Sufyan the leader of the Meccan forces did not want to fight that season, and wished to defer the fighting to another, season. So Abu Sufyan told a man named Nuam from a neutral tribe to ask the Prophet (PBUH) to suspend the war. The report of Nuam scared some of the Muslims, and there was an unwillingness to fight. The Prophet (PBUH) rejected this faint-hearted spirit and declared an oath that he would go to Badr, even if he went alone. Those brave utterance inspired them confidence and he was able to collect a force twice what he had had before.

The Prophet (PBUH) set out to Badr accompanied by 1500 fighters and 10 mounted horsemen, along with Ali ibn Abu Talib as the banner bearer. Abdullah ibn Rawahah was given authority over Medina during The Prophet's absence (PBUH). When the Muslims ariived at Badr, they stayed there waiting for the polytehists to come.

The Muslims, who were then at Badr, stayed for 8 days waiting for their enemy. They took advantage of their stay as they were selling goods and earning double as much the price out of it. When the idolaters declined to fight, the balance of powers swung to the benefit of the Muslims, who thus regained their military reputation, their dignity and managed to enforce their presence.

Abu Sufyan's forces comprised 2000 footmen and 50 horsemen. They reached Azzahran, some far from Mecca, and camped at a water place called Mijannah. Being hesitant, depressed and extremely terrified of the consequences of the looming fight, Abu Sufyan turned to his people and began to introduce cowardice-based, feeble pretexts in order to discourage his men from going to war, saying: "O tribe of Quraysh! Nothing will improve the condition you are in but a fruitful year — a year during which your animals feed on plants and bushes and give you milk to drink. And I see that this is a dry year, therefore I am going back now, and I recommend you to return with me." His army was also possessed of the same fears, they readily obeyed him without any hesitation.

Exalted is he says: "So they returned with favor from God and bounty, no harm having touched them. And they pursued the pleasure of God, and God is the possessor of great bounty"." فَانقَلَبُوا بِنِعْمَةٍ مِّنَ اللَّـهِ وَفَضْلٍ لَّمْ يَمْسَسْهُمْ سُوءٌ وَاتَّبَعُوا رِضْوَانَ اللَّـهِ، وَاللَّـهُ ذُو فَضْلٍ عَظِيمٍ" (3:174).

In this year: the Prophet (PBUH) ordered Zaid ibn Thabet to learn Torah, so he learnt it in 15 days.

God revealed: "And let the People of the Gospel judge by what God has revealed therein. And whoever does not judge by what God has revealed - then it is those who are the defiantly disobedient"." وَلْيَحْكُمْ أَهْلُ الْإِنجِيلِ بِمَا أَنزَلَ اللَّـهُ فِيهِ، وَمَن لَّمْ يَحْكُم بِمَا أَنزَلَ اللَّـهُ فَأُولَـٰئِكَ هُمُ الْفَاسِقُونَ" (5:47).

His marriage (PBUH) to Umm Salama

In this year, the Prophet (PBUH) married to Umm Salam in Shawwal.

During the Battle of Uhud, Abu Salama was severely injured. While Abu Salama was dying due to these wounds, he recalled a story to Umm Salama involving a message he had heard from the Prophet (PBUH): "I heard the Messenger of God saying, 'Whenever a calamity afflicts anyone he should say, "Surely from God we are and to Him we shall certainly return."' And he would pray, 'O Lord, give me in return something better from it which only You, Exalted and Mighty can give'". Her husband eventually died from the wounds he received in the Battle of Uhud. Umm Salama memorized the hadith recalled by her husband prior to his death, and began reciting the given prayer.

Following Abdullah ibn Abdulasad's death in the battle of Uhud, she became known as Ayyin Alarab - "The one who had lost her husband". She had no family in Medina except her small children, but she was given support by both the Muhajirun and Ansar. After finishing the iddah of four months and ten days, the sufficient amount of time that a woman must wait after the death of her husband before she can remarry, Umm Salama got offers of marriage. Abu Bakr and then Umar asked to marry her, but she declined. The Prophet (PBUH) himself then proposed to Umm Salama. She initially hesitated to accept, stating, "O Prophet (PBUH), I have three traits. I am a woman who is extremely jealous and I am afraid that you will see in me something that will anger you and cause God to punish me. I am a woman who is already advanced in age and I am a woman who has a young family."

However, The Prophet (PBUH) mollified each of her concerns, "Regarding the jealousy you mentioned, I pray to God the Almighty to let it go away from you. Regarding the question of age you have mentioned, I am afflicted with the same problem as you. Regarding the dependent family you have mentioned, your family is mine."

Tale of those who died in this year

- Alharith ibn Assamah ibn Amr ibn 'Attic, Abu Saad

He fought with the Prophet (PBUH) at Badr, then at Uhud and he was killed in the battle of Bir Maona.

- Haram ibn Milhan

During the Expedition of Bir Maona, Muslims sent a messenger (Haram ibn Milhan) with a letter of The Prophet (PBUH) to Amir ibn Tufayl, the cousin of Abu Bara and the chief of Banu Amir. Amir did not read the Message but rather ordered a man to spear Haram ibn Milhan in the back.

- Zainab bint Khuzayma

Zainab bint Khuzayma was one of the wives of the Prophet (PBUH), he married her in Ramadan in the 3rd Hijri year. She died during the month of Rabi' II in the 4th Hijri year. She was 30 years old when she died.

- Abdullah ibn Uthman ibn Affan, his mother is Rukaya, the daughter of the Prophet (PBUH):

He was born in Islam era, he reached six years. He died in Jummada I.

- Abu Salama; Abdullah ibn Abd Alasad Almakhzumi ibn Hillal ibn Makhzoum.

Abu Salama was one of the early companions of The Prophet (PBUH). He was born to Barrah Bint Abdulmutalib and Abdul

Asad, thus making him the first cousin of the Prophet (PBUH); as Barrah was the sister of Abdullah ibn Abdulmutalib, he was married to Umm Salama, and they were among the first who converted to Islam.

Abu Salama was also involved in the migration towards Abyssinia but later came back under the protection of his uncle Abu Talib ibn Abdulmutallib

Abu Salama died out of a wound he sustained during the Battle of Uhud that reopened after he had led the Expedition of Qatan. After his death, The Prophet (PBUH) married his widow.

- Amir ibn Fuhayra; Abu Amr

Amir ibn Fuhayra fought at Badr and Uhud but he was killed on the day of Bir Maona. He converted to Islam before entering of the Prophet (PBUH) into Dar ibn Alarqam.

- Asim ibn Thabut ibn Qais

He fought at Badr and Uhud but he was killed at the battle of Uhud.

- Fatimah bint Asad ibn Hashim, the mother of Ali ibn Abu Tali

(May God be pleased with them). She died in the 4th Hijri year.

Then, the 5th Hijri year

Some events:

- Expedition of Dhat Alriqa

The expedition of Dhat Alriqa took place in Muhharram.

Muhammed received the news that certain tribes of Banu Ghatafan were assembling at Dhat Alriqa with suspicious purposes.

The Prophet (PBUH) proceeded towards Nejd heading 400 or 700 men, after he had mandated Uthman ibn Affan for the affairs of Medina during his absence. The Muslim fighters penetrated deep into their land until they reached a spot called Nakhlah where they came across some bedouins of Ghatfan.

The Prophet (PBUH) made a surprise raid on them to disperse them. The Ghatafan fled to the mountains, leaving their women behind. No fighting took place but the Prophet (PBUH) attacked them and captured their women.

When the prayer time came, the Muslims were worried that the Ghatafan men might descend from their mountain hideaway and make a sudden attack on them while they were praying. For this fear, the Prophet (PBUH) introduced the 'service of prayer of danger.' In this arrangement, a party shall stand to guard while the other party prays. Then they take turns.

Expedition of Dumat Aljandal

It took place in Rabi' I. Dumat Aljandal is located at about a distance of fifteen-day-march from Medina and five from Damascus. The Prophet (PBUH) received news that some tribes, close to Dumat Aljandal, on the borders of Syria, were involved in a road robbery and looting, and were on their way to gather troops and attack Medina. He immediately appointed ibn Arfatah Alghifari to manage the affairs of Medina during his absence, and left, heading a thousand Muslims, a man named Madhkur, from Banu Udhrah, was his guide. On their way to Dumat Aljandal, they used to march by night and hide by day, so that they might surprise the enemy.

When they drew near their destination, the Muslims discovered that the highway men had moved to another place, so they captured their cattle and shepherds. The Prophet (PBUH) stayed there for 5 days during which he sent expeditionary forces to hunt for the enemy fighters but they detected none.

In this year, the Prophet (PBUH) sent money for Quraysh as they suffered a terrible year.

Envoy of Saad ibn Bakr

Ibn Abbas reported: Banu Saad ibn Bakr sent Damam ibn Thaalabah to the Prophet of God (PBUH). He came to him and made his camel kneel down near the gate of the mosque. He then tied its leg and entered the mosque. The narrator then reported in a similar way. Then he said; 'Which of you is The Prophet

(PBUH)?' He was resting among them, and we said to him: 'This white man who is reclining.' The man said to him: 'O son of Abdulkuttalib' The Prophet (PBUH) said to him: 'I have answered you.' The man said: 'O Prophet of God (PBUH), I am going to ask you questions and I will be harsh in asking.' He said; 'Ask whatever you like.' The man said; 'I adjure you by your Lord, and the Lord of those who came before you, has God sent you to all the people?' The Prophet (PBUH) said: 'by God, yes,' He said: 'I adjure you by God, has God commanded you to fast this month each year?' The Prophet (PBUH) said: "Yes". He replied: 'I adjure you by God, has God commanded you to take this charity from our rich and divide it among our poor?' The Prophet (PBUH) said: 'By God, Yes.' Then he said; 'I believe in that which you have brought, and I am the envoy of my people who are coming after me. I am Dimam ibn Thalabah, the brother of Banu Saad ibn Bakr."

In this year Banu Muzaina sent a delegation

Banu Muzaina, first, sent 400 men in Rajab in the 5th Hijri year. The Prophet (PBUH) commended them to return to their people as they were migrants while they were among their people.

Expedition of Almuraysi

It was an early Muslim campaign against the tribe of Banu Mustaliq which took place in Shaaban.

Banu Mustaliq was staying near to a well called Almuraysi; they gathered and wanted to launch a war against the Prophet (PBUH). The Prophet knew about that so he sent them Buraydah ibn Alhusaib to explore the matter and make sure of that; he met Alharith ibn Abu Dherar. Buraydah returned to the Prophet (PBUH) after being certain of the accurateness of the news. The Prophet called people for them and entrusted Zaid ibn Haritha to dispose the affairs of Medina. The Prophet (PBUH) went out together with his companions on Monday, the 2nd Shaaban.

On hearing about the arrival of the Muslims, the tribe was terrified, and the Arabs that accompanied them changed sides and fled for their lives. Abu Bakr was entrusted as the commander of the Migrants, and Saad ibn Ubadah was the commander of the Ansar. The two armies were stationed at a well called Almuraysi, near the sea, a short distance from Mecca. They fought with bows and arrows for an hour, and then the Muslims advanced so rapidly, they surrounded the Almustaliq and took the entire tribe as prisoners, with their families, herds and flock. The battle ended with full victory for the Muslims.

Two hundred families were taken as captives, two hundred camels, five thousand sheep, goats, as well as a huge quantity of household goods which were captured as booty. Only one Muslim was killed by mistake by a man from the Ansars.

Juwayriyah bint Alharith, daughter of the Banu Almustaliq chief was one of the captives, and agreed to marry Muḥammad in exchange for releasing 100 prisoners who converted to Islam, as recompense.

Aisha, narrated: 'Juwayriyyah, daughter of Alharith ibn Almustaliq, fell to the lot of Thabut ibn Qays ibn Shammas, or to her cousin. She entered into an agreement to purchase her freedom. She was a very beautiful woman.

Aisha said: She then came to the Prophet (PBUH) asking him for the purchase of her freedom. When she was standing at the door, I looked at her with disapproval. I realised that the Prophet (PBUH) would look at her in the same way that I had looked.

She said: Prophet (PBUH), I am Juwayriyyah, daughter of Alharith, and something has happened to me, which is known to you. I have fallen to the lot of Thabet ibn Qays ibn Shammas, and I have entered into an agreement to purchase of my freedom. I have come to you to seek assistance for the purchase of my freedom.

The Prophet (PBUH) said: Are you inclined to that which is better? She asked: What is that, Prophet (PBUH)? He replied: I shall pay the price of your freedom on your behalf, and I shall marry you.

She said: I shall do this. She (Aisha) said: The people then heard that the Prophet (PBUH) had married Juwayriyyah. They released the captives in their possession and set them free, and said: They are the relatives of the Prophet (PBUH) by marriage. We did not see any woman greater than Juwayriyyah who brought blessings to her people. One hundred families of Banu Almustaliq were set free on account of her.

The revelation of the Verse of Tayammum

Aisha, the wife of the Prophet (PBUH), narrated: 'We set out with The Prophet (PBUH) on one of his journeys, and when we were at Baida, a necklace of mine was broken (and lost). The Prophet (PBUH) stayed there to look for it, and so did the people along with him. Neither were they at a place of water, nor did they have any water with them. So the people went to Abu Bakr and said, "Don't you see what `Aisha has done? She has made The Prophet (PBUH) and the people, stay where there is no water and they have no water with them." Abu Bakr came while the Prophet (PBUH) was sleeping with his head on my thigh. He said (to me), "You have detained the Prophet (PBUH) and the people where there is no water, and they have no water with them." So he admonished me and said what God wished him to say, and he hit me on my flanks. Nothing prevented me from moving (because of pain! but the position of The Prophet (PBUH) on my thigh. So The Prophet (PBUH) got up when dawn broke and there was no water, so God revealed the Verse of Tayammum. Usaid ibn Hudair said, "It is not the first blessing of yours, O the family of

Abu Bakr." Then we made the camel on which I was riding, got up, and found the necklace under it.'

Aisha also narrated: "Whenever the Prophet (PBUH) intended to go on a journey; he would draw lots amongst his wives and would take with him the one upon whom the lot fell. During an expedition, he drew lots amongst us and the lot fell upon me, and I proceeded with him after God had decreed the use of the veil by women. I was carried in a Howdaj (on the camel) and dismounted while still in it. When the Prophet (PBUH) was through with his expedition and returned home, and we approached the city of Medina, the Prophet (PBUH) ordered us to proceed at night. When the order of departure was given, I walked till I was past the army to defecate. After finishing I returned (to the camp) to depart (with the others) and suddenly realized that my necklace over my chest was missing. So, I returned to look for it and I was late because of that. The people, who used to carry me on the camel, came to my Howdaj and put it on the back of the camel, thinking that I was in it.

As, at that time, I was of little weight, thin and lean, and did not use to eat much. So, those people did not feel the difference in the heaviness of the Howdaj while lifting it, and they put it over the camel. At that time I was a young lady. They set the camel moving and proceeded on. I found my necklace after the army had gone, and came to their camp to find nobody.

So, I went to the place where I used to stay, thinking that they would discover my absence and come back.

While in that state, I felt drowsy and slept. Safwan ibn Muattal Assulami Alzakawany was behind the army and reached my residence in the morning. When he met a sleeping person, he came to me, and he used to see me before veiling. So, I got up when I heard him. He made his camel knell down. He got down from his camel, and put his leg on the front legs of the camel and then I rode and sat over it. Safwan set out walking, leading the camel by the rope till we reached the army who had halted to take rest at midday. Then whoever was meant for destruction, fell into destruction, (some people accused me falsely) and the leader of the false accusers was Abdullah ibn Ubai ibn Salul. After that we returned to Medina, and I became ill for one month while the people were spreading the forged statements of the false accusers. I was feeling during my ailment as if I were not receiving the usual kindness from the Prophet (PBUH) which I used to receive from him when I got sick. But he would come, greet and say, 'How is that (girl)?' I did not know anything of what was going on till I recovered from my ailment and went out with Um Mistah to the Manasi where we used to defecate, and we used not to go to defecate except from night to night and that was before we had toilets near to our houses. And this habit of ours was similar to the the habit of the old 'Arabs in the open country (or away from houses).

So, I and Um Mistah bint Ruhm went out walking. Um Mistah stumbled because of her long dress and on that she said, 'Let Mistah be ruined.' I said, 'You are saying a bad word. Why are you abusing a man who took part in (the battle of) Badr?' She said, 'O Hanata (you there) didn't you hear what they said?' Then she told me the rumors of the false accusers. My sickness was aggravated, and when I returned home, the Prophet (PBUH) came to me, and after greeting he said, 'How is that (girl)?' I requested him to allow me to go to my parents. I wanted then to be sure of the news through them, the Prophet (PBUH) allowed me.

I went to my parents and asked my mother, 'What are the people talking about me?' She said, 'O my daughter! Don't worry much about this matter. By God, never is there a charming woman loved by her husband who has other wives, but the women would forge false news about her.' I said, 'Glorified be God! Are the people really talking about this matter?' That night I kept on weeping and could not sleep till morning.

In the morning, the Prophet (PBUH) called Ali ibn Abu Talib and Usama ibn Zaid when the Divine Inspiration delayed, to consul them about divorcing his wife (i.e. Aisha). Usama ibn Zaid said what he knew of the good reputation of his wives and added, 'O the Prophet (PBUH)! Keep you wife, for, by God, we know nothing about her but good.' Ali ibn Abu Talib said, 'O the Prophet (PBUH)! God has no imposed restrictions on you, and there are many women other than her, yet you may ask the maid who will tell you the truth.'

On that the Prophet (PBUH) called Buraira and said, 'O Buraira. Did you ever see anything which roused your suspicions about her?' Buraira said, 'No, by God Who has sent you with the truth, I have never seen in her anything faulty except that she is a girl of immature age, who sometimes sleeps and leaves the dough for the goats to eat.' On that day the Prophet (PBUH) ascended the pulpit and requested that somebody support him in punishing Abdullah ibn Ubai ibn Salul. The Prophet said, 'Who will support me to punish that person (`Abdullah ibn Ubai ibn Salul) who has hurt me by slandering the reputation of my family? By God, I know nothing about my family but good, and they have accused a person about whom I know nothing except good, and he never entered my house except in my company.' Saad ibn Moaaz got up and said, 'O Prophet of God (PBUH)! By God, I will relieve you from him. If that man is from the tribe of the Aws, then we will chop his head off, and if he is from our brothers, the Khazraj, then order us, and we will fulfill your order.' On that Saad ibn Ubada, the chief of the Khazraj and before this incident, he had been a pious man, got up, motivated by his zeal for his tribe and said, 'By God, you have told a lie; you cannot kill him, and you will never be able to kill him.' On that Usaid ibn Alhadir got up and said (to

Saad ibn Ubada), 'By God! You are a liar. By God, we will kill him; and you are a hypocrite, defending the hypocrites.'

Accordingly, the two tribes of Aws and Khazraj got excited and were about to fight each other, while the Prophet (PBUH) was standing on the pulpit. He got down and quieted them till they became silent and he kept quiet.

On that day I kept on weeping so much so that neither did my tears stop, nor could I sleep. In the morning, my parents were with me and I had wept for two nights and a day, till I thought my liver would burst from weeping.

While they were sitting with me and I was weeping, an Ansari woman asked my permission to enter, and I allowed her to come in. She sat down and started weeping with me. While we were in this state, the Prophet (PBUH) came and sat down and he had never sat with me since the day they forged the accusation. No revelation regarding my case came to him for a month. Then he said, 'O `Aisha! I have been informed such-and-such about you; if you are innocent, then God will soon reveal your innocence, and if you have committed a sin, then repent to God and ask Him to forgive you, for when a person confesses his sin and asks God for forgiveness, God accepts his repentance.'

When the Prophet (PBUH) finished his speech, my tears ceased completely and there remained not even a single drop of it. I requested my father to reply to the Prophet (PBUH) on my behalf. My father said, By God, I do not know what to say to the Prophet (PBUH).' I said to my mother, 'Talk to the Prophet (PBUH) on my behalf.' She said, 'By God, I do not know what to say to the Prophet (PBUH) . I was a young girl and did not have much knowledge of the Qur'an. I said. 'I know, by God, that you have listened to what people are saying and that has been planted in your minds and you have taken it as a truth. Now, if I told you that I am innocent and God knows that I am innocent, you would not believe me and if I confessed to you falsely that I am guilty, and God knows that I am innocent you would believe me. By God, I don't compare my situation with you except to the situation of Joseph's father (i.e. Jacob) who said: "So patience is most fitting. And God is the one sought for help against that which you describe"." "فَصَبْرٌ جَمِيلٌ وَاللَّهُ الْمُسْتَعَانُ عَلَىٰ مَا تَصِفُونَ" (12:18)

Then, I turned to the other side of my bed hoping that God would prove my innocence. By God I never thought that God would reveal Divine Inspiration in my case, as I considered myself too inferior to be talked of in the Holy Qur'an. I had hoped that the Prophet (PBUH) might have a dream in which God would prove my innocence. By God, the Prophet (PBUH) had not got up and nobody had left the house before the Divine Inspiration came to the Prophet . So, there overtook him the same state which used to overtake him, (when he used to have, on being inspired divinely). He was sweating so much so that the drops of the sweat were dropping like pearls though it was a (cold) wintry day. When that state of the Prophet (PBUH) was over, he was smiling and the first word he said, `Aisha! Thank God, for God has declared your innocence.' My mother told me to go to the Prophet (PBUH). I replied, 'By God I will not go to him and will not thank but God.' So God revealed: "Indeed, those who came with falsehood are a group among you"."إِنَّ الَّذِينَ جَاءُوا بِالْإِفْكِ عُصْبَةٌ مِّنكُمْ" (24.11). When God gave the declaration of my Innocence.

Abu Bakr, who used to provide for Mistah ibn Uthatha for he was his relative, said, 'By God, I will never provide Mistah with anything because of what he said about Aisha.' But God later revealed: "And let not those of virtue among you and wealth swear not to give [aid] to their relatives and the needy and the emigrants for the cause of God, and let them pardon and overlook. Would you not like that God should forgive you? And God is Forgiving and Merciful"." وَلَا يَأْتَلِ أُولُو الْفَضْلِ مِنكُمْ وَالسَّعَةِ أَن يُؤْتُوا أُولِي الْقُرْبَىٰ وَالْمَسَاكِينَ وَالْمُهَاجِرِينَ فِي سَبِيلِ اللَّـهِ، وَلْيَعْفُوا وَلْيَصْفَحُوا، أَلَا تُحِبُّونَ أَن يَغْفِرَ اللَّـهُ لَكُمْ، وَاللَّـهُ غَفُورٌ رَّحِيمٌ" (24:22)

After that Abu Bakr said, 'Yes! By God! I like that God should forgive me,' and resumed helping Mistah whom he used to help before.

The Prophet (PBUH) also asked Zainab bint Jahsh (i.e. the Prophet's wife about me saying, 'What do you know and what did you see?' She replied, 'O the Prophet (PBUH)! I refrain to claim hearing or seeing what I have not heard or seen. By God, I know nothing except goodness about Aisha." Aisha further added "Zainab was competing with me (in her beauty and the Prophet's love), yet God protected her (from being malicious), for she had piety."

His marriage (PBUH) to Zainab bint Jahsh

In this year, the Prophet (PBUH) married to Zainab bint Jahsh, her mother is Umama bint Abdulmutalib, Zainab's father was Jahsh ibn Riyab, an immigrant from the Asad ibn Khuzayma tribe who had settled in Mecca under the protection of the Umayya clan. Zainab, who had become a muslim was among those who attended her brother Abdullah on the Hijra to Medina. Zainab married his adopted son, Zaid ibn Harithah, she was a very beautiful woman. Zainab at first refused the proposal but then agreed and married Zaid. The Prophet (PBUH) married to Zainab in this year when she was 35 years old.

Aisha narrated (May God be pleased with her): "If the Prophet (PBUH) was to have concealed anything that was revealed to him, then he would have concealed these verses: " And [remember, O The Prophet (PBUH)], when you said to the one on whom God bestowed favor and you bestowed favor, "Keep your wife and fear God," while you concealed within yourself that which God is to disclose. And you feared the people, while God has more right that you fear Him. So when Zaid had no longer any need for her, We married her to you in order that there not be upon the believers any discomfort concerning the wives of their adopted sons when they no longer have need of them. And ever is the command of God accomplished"." وَإِذْ تَقُولُ لِلَّذِي أَنْعَمَ اللَّـهُ عَلَيْهِ وَأَنْعَمْتَ عَلَيْهِ أَمْسِكْ عَلَيْكَ زَوْجَكَ وَاتَّقِ اللَّـهَ وَتُخْفِي فِي نَفْسِكَ مَا اللَّـهُ مُبْدِيهِ وَتَخْشَى النَّاسَ وَاللَّـهُ أَحَقُّ أَن تَخْشَاهُ فَلَمَّا قَضَىٰ زَيْدٌ مِّنْهَا وَطَرًا زَوَّجْنَاكَهَا لِكَيْ لَا يَكُونَ عَلَى الْمُؤْمِنِينَ حَرَجٌ فِي أَزْوَاجِ أَدْعِيَائِهِمْ إِذَا قَضَوْا مِنْهُنَّ وَطَرًا، وَكَانَ أَمْرُ اللَّـهِ مَفْعُولً" (33:37).' They said: 'He married his wife's son, so God has revealed: "The Prophet (PBUH) is not the father of [any] one of your men, but [he is] the Prophet (PBUH) and last of the prophets. And ever is God, of all things, Knowing"." مَّا كَانَ مُحَمَّدٌ أَبَا أَحَدٍ مِّن رِّجَالِكُمْ وَلَـٰكِن رَّسُولَ اللَّـهِ وَخَاتَمَ النَّبِيِّينَ، وَكَانَ اللَّـهُ بِكُلِّ شَيْءٍ عَلِيمًا" (33:40). The Prophet (PBUH) had adopted him as a son when he was young, and he remained being called 'Zaid ibn The Prophet (PBUH)' until he grew up to adulthood, then God revealed: "Call them by [the names of] their fathers; it is more just in the sight of God. But if you do not know their fathers - then they are [still] your brothers in religion and those entrusted to you. And there is no blame upon you for that in which you have erred but [only for] what your hearts intended. And ever is God Forgiving and Merciful"." ادْعُوهُمْ لِآبَائِهِمْ هُوَ أَقْسَطُ عِندَ اللَّـهِ، فَإِن لَّمْ تَعْلَمُوا آبَاءَهُمْ فَإِخْوَانُكُمْ فِي الدِّينِ وَمَوَالِيكُمْ، وَلَيْسَ عَلَيْكُمْ جُنَاحٌ فِيمَا أَخْطَأْتُم بِهِ وَلَـٰكِن مَّا تَعَمَّدَتْ قُلُوبُكُمْ، وَكَانَ اللَّـهُ غَفُورًا رَّحِيمًا" (33:40).

Anas (God be pleased with him) reported: "When the 'Iddah of Zainab was over, God's Messenger (PBUH) said to Zaid to make a mention to her about him. Zaid went on until he came to her and she was fermenting her flour. He (Zaid) said: 'As I saw her I felt in my heart an idea of her greatness so much so that I could not see towards her (simply for the fact) that God's Messenger (PBUH) had made a mention of her. So I turned my back towards her and I turned upon my heels, and said: Zainab, God's Messenger (PBUH) has sent (me) with a message to you. She said: 'I do not do anything until I solicit the will of my Lord'. So she stood at her place of worship and the (verse of) the Qur'an (pertaining to her marriage) were revealed, and God's Messenger (PBUH) came to her without permission. He (the narrator) said: I saw that God's Messenger (PBUH) served us bread and meat."

Because of Zainab, Verses of Veiling revealed

Anas said that he was ten years old when the Prophet (PBUH) came to Medina. He said, "My mother decided that I would serve him and I served him for ten years. He died when I was twenty. I am the person who knows best about the business of the veil. The first instance that was revealed occurred when the Prophet (PBUH) built a room for Zainab bint Jahsh. He celebrated the wedding there, invited the people who came, ate and then left. A group remained with the Prophet, may God bless him and grant him peace. They stayed for a long time and then the Prophet went out and I went out hoping that they would leave. He walked and I walked with him until he came to the threshold of Aisha's room. Then, thinking that they would have left, he returned and I returned with him. He went to Zainab but they were still sitting there. He left again and I left with him until he once more reached the threshold of Aisha's room. When he thought that they would have gone, he went back again and I went back with him. This time they had indeed left. The Prophet, may God bless him and grant him peace, then put up a curtain between me and him, and the veil was revealed."

In this year, Battle of the Trench (Battle of the Confederates) occurred,

It had occurred in Dhul Qi'dah.

The reason for this battle was to defend Medina from attack, Banu Nadir and Banu Qaynuqa went to Mecca where they met with the leaders of Quraysh and provoked them to make war against the Prophet; Banu Nadir met with Quraysh of Mecca. Huyayy ibn Akhtab, along with other leaders from Khaybar, travelled to pledge allegiance with Safwan ibn Umayya at Mecca. Then, they joined Banu Ghatafan by paying them half of their harvest. Banu Assad also agreed to join, led by Tuleha Asadi. From Banu Sulaym, Nadir secured 700 men.

Other tribes included Banu Murra, with 400 men led by Hars ibn Auf Murri, and the Banu Shuja, with 700 men led by Sufyan ibn Abd Shams. In total, the power of the Confederate armies, although not agreed upon by scholars, is expected to have included about 10,000 men and six hundred horsemen. The army, which was led by Abu Sufyan, paraded, directing to Medina.

When the Prophet (PBUH) learnt about their gathering, he assembled the people of Medina to discuss the best approach of overcoming the enemy.

Ultimately, the outstripped Muslims opted to engage in a defending battle by digging deep trenches to act as a barrier along the northern front. The trick of a defensive trench was presented by Salman Alfarisi. Every capable Muslim in Medina including the Prophet (PBUH) contributed in digging the huge trench in six days. The trench was dug on the northern side only, as the rest of Medina was hemmed in rocky mountains and trees, impenetrable to large armies. All those who were with the Prophet at the Trench were 3000 men of Muslims. The Prophet called Abdullah ibn Umm Maktoum to manage the affairs of Medina.

The Prophet (PBUH) established his military center at the hillock of Sala' and the army was grouped there; this position would give the Muslims a benefit if the enemy crossed the trench. The army that would protect the city from the assault consisted of

3,000 men, and included all residents of Medina over the age of 14.

It is narrated that the Prophet (PBUH) participated with them while digging the trenches. While they were digging the trench, there was a great rock that they could not move, the Prophet (PBUH) took an ax and asked help from God and poked the rock till it was destroyed.

Scholars said that the Prophet (PBUH) went out on Monday the 8th of Dhul Qi'dah. The banner of the migrants was held by Zaid ibn Haritha and that of the Ansar was held by Saad ibn Ubada.

Abu Sufyan sent Huyayy ibn Akhtab to Banu Quraiza. Huyayy eventually managed to enter and convince them that the Muslims would surely be amazed. Moreover, the scene of the massive Confederate armies, stepping the ground with soldiers and horses turned Quraiza opinion in the favour of the Confederacy.

In addition, news of the Quraiza's supposed rejection of the pact with The Prophet (PBUH) spread, and Umar promptly informed The Prophet (PBUH) of the same. Such suspicions were strengthened by the movement of enemy troops towards the sanctuaries of Quraiza. Accordingly, the Prophet (PBUH) became worried about their conduct and realised the serious danger Quraiza posed. The Prophet (PBUH) warned against spreading the news of a potential breach of the pact on Quraiza's part, so as to avoid any panic within Muslim ranks, the Prophet (PBUH) tried to hide his knowledge of the actions of Banu Quraiza; yet, rumors soon spread of a massive assault on the city of Medina from Quraiza's side which severely disheartened the people of Medina. The situation was very hard and fear was great as what God has revealed: "[Remember] when they came at you from above you and from below you, and when eyes shifted [in fear], and hearts reached the throats and you assumed about God [various] assumptions"." إِذْ جَاءُوكُم مِّن فَوْقِكُمْ وَمِنْ أَسْفَلَ مِنكُمْ وَإِذْ زَاغَتِ الْأَبْصَارُ وَبَلَغَتِ الْقُلُوبُ الْحَنَاجِرَ وَتَظُنُّونَ بِاللَّهِ الظُّنُونَا" (33:10).

The Prophet (PBUH) sent a letter to Ghatafan offering them a third of Medina's harvest if they withdrew. Although the Ghatafan asked for the half, they eventually agreed to negotiate with The Prophet (PBUH) on those terms. Before the Prophet (PBUH) began drafting the agreement, he consulted the Medinan leaders. They greatly refused the terms of the agreement, claiming that Medina had never fallen to such levels of humiliation. The negotiations did not complete.

Then, violent winds blew out the camp fires, depriving the Confederate army of their source of heat. God, Exalted is He, has revealed: "And Allah repelled those who disbelieved, in their rage, not having obtained any good. And sufficient was Allah for the believers in battle, and ever is Allah Powerful and Exalted in

Might.". " وَرَدَّ اللَّهُ الَّذِينَ كَفَرُوا بِغَيْظِهِمْ لَمْ يَنَالُوا خَيْرًا ۚ وَكَفَى اللَّهُ الْمُؤْمِنِينَ الْقِتَالَ ۚ وَكَانَ اللَّهُ قَوِيًّا عَزِيزًا" (33:25).

It was reported that the confederates strolled around the trench for several, the leaders of the army opted to pass through the narrowest point at the trench and they managed to pass through it but there were fighting among them and Muslims managed to kill some of them and other returned and fled. Ali (may God be pleased with him) managed to kill Amr ibn Wud.

They promised that they would return in the morning and they fought all the day till the evening and they returned defeated.

The provisions of the Confederate armies were finishing. Horses and camels were dying because of hunger and their injuries. For these days when the weather had been extremely cold and wet for the enemy, whose camps were blown by the winds, the Muslim camp, on the other hand, was shielded from such violent winds. The enemy's tents were torn up, their fires were extinguished, as well as the sand and rain demolished their faces, and they were frightened by these negative signs. During the night, the Confederate armies retreated, all enemy forces evacuated the land, none of their camps remained.

The Prophet (PBUH) and his companions were in siege for ten and some scholars said that it was for 24 days.

The Prophet received a visit from Nuaym ibn Masud, an Arab leader who was well respected by the entire confederacy, but he secretly converted to Islam. The Prophet (PBUH) asked him to end the siege by generating a disagreement amongst Confederates.

Nuaym then came up with an efficient strategy. He first went to the Banu Quraiza and warned them about the plans of the rest of the Confederacy. If the siege fails, he said, the Confederacy will not be afraid to leave the Jews, leaving them for the Prophet (PBUH). Quraiza should thus demand Confederate leaders as hostages in return for cooperation. This frightened Quraiza.

Then, Nuaym went to Abu Sufyan, the Confederate leader, warning him that Quraiza had change sides to the Prophet (PBUH). He stated that the tribe intended to ask the Confederacy for hostages, in return for cooperation, but certainly to hand over to the Prophet (PBUH). Thus the Confederacy should not give a single man as hostage. Nuaym repeated the same message to other tribes in the Confederacy.

Nuaym's trick worked and after consulting, the Confederate leaders sent Ikrimah to Quraiza, indicating a united invasion of Medina. Quraiza, however, demanded hostages as a guarantee that the Confederacy would not desert them. The Confederacy, considered that Quraiza might give the hostage to the Prophet (PBUH), and refused. Messages were sent back and forth between the parties, but each held to its position persistently. It was said that when each confederate feared the betrayal of the other; Banu

Quraiza excused by Saturday. During the night of Saturday, there was a severe wind, then, Abu Sufyan declared his withdrawal and advised them to do the same as him.

It has been narrated by Ibrahim Altaimi, upon his father who said: "We were sitting in the company of Hudhaifa. A man said: If I were in the time of the Messenger of God (PBUH), I would have fought by his side and would have striven hard for his causes. Hudhaifa said: You might have done that, (but you should not make a flourish of your enthusiasm). I was with the Messenger of God (PBUH) on the night of the Battle of the Confederates and we were caught by a violent wind and severe cold. The Messenger of God (PBUH) said: Hark, the man who brings me the news of the enemy shall be ranked with me on the Day of Judgment by God (the Glorious and Exalted). We all kept quiet and none of us responded to him. (Again) he said: Hark, a man who brings me the news of the enemy shall be ranked with me on the Day of Judgment by God (the Glorious and Exalted). We kept quiet and none of us responded to him. He again said: Hark, a man who brings me the news of the enemy shall be ranked with me on the Day of Judgment by God (the Glorious and Exalted) Then he said: Get up Hudhaifa, bring me the news of the enemy. When he called me by name I had no alternative but to get up. He said: Go and bring me information about the enemy, and do nothing that may provoke them against me. When I left him, I felt warm as if I were walking in a heated bath until I reached them.

I saw Abu Sufyan warming his back against fire I put an arrow in the middle of the bow, intending to shoot at him, when I recalled the words of the Messenger of God (PBUH) "Do not provoke them against me." Had I shot at him, I would have hit him. But I returned and felt warm as if I were walking in a heated bath. Presenting myself to him, I gave him information about the enemy. When I had done so, I began to feel cold, so the Messenger of God (PBUH) wrapped me in a blanket that he had in excess to his own requirement and with which he used to cover himself while saying his prayers. So I continued to sleep until it was morning. When it was morning he said: Get up, O heavy sleeper.

It is said that 6 men from Muslims and 3 men from infidels were killed at the trench.

Invasion of Banu Quraiza occurred in this year

It occurred in Dhul Qi'da. Banu Quraiza initially told the Muslims that they were allied to them during the Battle of the Trench, however, later they sided with the polytheists of Quraysh and their allies. Jewish leaders organized efforts against the Prophet (PBUH) and the Muslims. Three Jewish leaders from the tribe of Banu Nadir, three Jewish leaders from the tribe of Wa'il, and various other Jewish groups and leaders united and pressured Banu Quraiza to betray their agreement to The Prophet (PBUH).

During the Battle of the Trench, when the Muslims were surrounded by a large hostile force, Banu Quraiza joined the enemies of the Muslims and threatened the Muslims from within the town itself.

It is narrated that the Prophet (PBUH) was asked by Gabriel to launch a raid against Banu Quraiza.

The Messenger of God returned to Medina in triumph and the people put down their weapons. While the Messenger of God was washing off the dust of battle in the house of Umm Salamah, may God be pleased with her, Gabriel, came to him wearing a turban of brocade, riding on a mule on which was a cloth of silk brocade. He said, "Have you put down your weapons, O Messenger of God" He said, "Yes" He said, "But the angels have not put down theirs. I have just now come back from pursuing the people." Then he said: "God, may He be blessed and exalted, commands you to get up and go to Banu Quraiza. According to another report, "What a fighter you are! Have you put down your weapons" He said, "Yes". He said, "But we have not put down our weapons yet, get up and go to these people." He said: "Where?" He said, "Banu Quraiza, for God has commanded me to shake them." So the Messenger of God got up immediately, and commanded the people to march towards Banu Quraiza, who were a few miles from Medina. This was after the prayer of noon. He said, No one among you should pray Asr (afternoon) except at Banu Quraiza.

The Prophet entitled ibn Umm Maktoum to manage the affairs of Medina and he went out together with 3000 men on Wednesday, the 7th of Dhul Qi'da and sieged them for 15 days and some scholars said the siege was for 25 nights.

When they reached the dwellings of Banu Quraiza, they laid tight siege to their forts. Banu Quraiza retreated into their fortress and endured the siege for 25 days. When their spirit faded, Kaab ibn Asad (the chief of the tribe) suggested three alternative ways out of their dilemma: embrace Islam, kill their own children and women, then rush out for a charge to either win or die; or make a surprise attack on the Sabbath. None of these alternatives was accepted by Banu Quraiza. Instead, they asked to confer with Abu Lubaba, one of their allies from Aws. Abu Lubaba felt pity for the women and children of the tribe who were crying and when he was asked whether Quraiza should surrender to The Prophet (PBUH), he advised them to do so. Though he also "made a sign with his hand toward his throat, indicating that their fate would be slaughter". Abu Lubab begged The Prophet (PBUH) for forgiveness, on behalf of the Quraiza, but The Prophet (PBUH) said it is only God who can forgive him.

On the following morning, Banu Quraiza surrendered and the Muslims seized their stronghold and their stores. 1500 swords, 2000 spears, 300 armours and 500 shields, were seized by The Prophet (PBUH).

After their barracks were stormed by Ali, they had no choice but to comply with The Prophet (PBUH)'s judgement. The Prophet (PBUH) ordered that the men should be cuffed, while the women and children were separated in confinement. Consequently Aws tribe hurried asking the Prophet (PBUH) to be tolerant towards them. He suggested that Saad ibn Muaz, should decide their fate.

When Saad arrived, his fellow Aws pleaded for forgiveness, on the benefit of Quraiza. He then pronounced that "The men should be killed, the property divided, and the women and children taken as captives". The Prophet (PBUH) approved of the ruling, calling it similar to God's judgment. Trenches were dug in Medina and about six to seven hundred Jewish men were beheaded therein.

Tale of those died in this year.

- Thaalabah ibn Ghanamah ibn Adi ibn Sinan

He witnessed Alaqaba with the seventy men. He fought at Badr and the Trench and he was killed then.

- Julaibib

With Julaybib in mind, The Prophet (PBUH) went to an Ansari man and said: "I want to have your daughter married." "How wonderful and blessed, O Messenger of God and what a delight to the eye (this would be)," he replied. "I do not want her for myself," added The Prophet (PBUH). "Then for whom, O Messenger of

God?" asked the man, obviously disappointed. "For Julaibib," said The Prophet (PBUH). The Ansari went to consult with his wife, telling her of The Prophet (PBUH)'s desire for their daughter to marry Julaibiib. His wife rejected, and protested saying "To Julaibib! No, never to Julaibib! No, by God, we shall not marry (her) to him."

While he was preparing to inform The Prophet (PBUH) of what his wife said, the daughter hearing her mother's protestations, asked: "Who has asked you to marry me?", she was told that the Messenger of God wants her hand in marriage for Julaibiibn. As the Mother continued her crying and wailing, the daughter spoke said, "O my Mother fear God, think of what you are saying, are you turning away the Messenger of God.'O my Mother it does not suit a believer to make their own decision once God and his Messenger have decided on a matter. Do you think that the Messenger of God will disgrace us?"

Abu Barza reported that the Prophet (PBUH) was there in a battlefield that God conferred upon him the spoils of war. He said to his Companions: "Is anyone missing amongst you? They said: So and so and so. He again said: Is there anyone missing amongst you? They said: So and so and so. He then said: Is there anyone missing amongst you? They said: No. Thereupon the Prophet said: But I am missing Julaibiib,They (his Companions) searched him amongst those who had been killed and they found him by the side of seven (dead bodies) whom he had killed and he had been killed (by the opponents). The Prophet (PBUH) came there and stood (by his side) and said: He killed seven (persons). Then (his opponents) killed him. He is mine and I am his. He then placed him upon his hands and there was none else to lift but the Prophet (PBUH). Then the grave was dug for him and he was placed in the grave and no mention is made of a bath.

- Khalad ibn Suwaid ibn Thaalabah ibn Amr ibn Harithah

He witnessed Aqaba and he fought at Badr, the Trench and the invasion of Banu Quraiza, he was killed then. There was a woman from Banu Quraiza who throw a stone on his head and he died.

Aisha (May God be pleased with her) narrated: "No woman of Banu Quraiza was killed except one. She was with me, talking and laughing on her back and belly (extremely), while the Messenger of God (PBUH) was killing her people with the swords. Suddenly a man called her name: Where is so-and-so? She said: I am. He asked: What is the matter with you? She said: I did a new act The man took her and beheaded her.

Saad ibn Moaz ibn Alnu'man ibn 'Imru' Alqais, of Abdul Ashhal clan of the Aws tribe, Abu Amr. His mother is Kabsha bint Rafi. He was the chief of Aws tribe in Medina. He converted at the hands of Mu'sab ibn Umair. His conversion led to the immediate conversion of his entire subtribe of the Aws, Banu Abdul Ashhal. The banner of Aws was held by Saad ibn Mu'z at Badr.

He fought at Uhud and stood beside the Prophet (PBUH) when others fled. He was injured at the Trench.

`Aisha (May God be pleased with her) narrated: "Saad was wounded on the day of Khandaq (i.e. Trench) when a man from Quraysh, called Hibban ibn Al`araqa hit him (with an arrow). The was from (the tribe of) Banu Mais ibn 'Amir ibn Lu'ai who shot an arrow at Saad's medial arm vein. The Prophet (PBUH) pitched a tent (for Saad) in the Mosque so that he might be near to the Prophet (PBUH) to visit." When the Prophet returned from the battle of Trench and laid down his arms and took a bath. Gabriel came to him and said, "You have laid down the arms?" By God, I have not laid them down. Go out to them (to attack them)." The Prophet (PBUH) said, "Where?" Gabriel pointed towards Banu Quraiza. So God's Messenger (PBUH) went to them (i.e. Banu Quraiza) (i.e. besieged them). They then surrendered to the Prophet's judgment but he directed them to Saad to give his verdict concerning them. Saad said, "I give my judgment that their warriors should be killed, their women and children should be taken as captives, and their properties distributed."

Jabir narrated: "I heard the Prophet (PBUH) saying, "The Throne (of God) shook at the death of Saad ibn Moaaz." Through another group of narrators, Jabir added, "I heard the Prophet (PBUH) saying, 'The Throne of the Beneficent shook because of the death of Saad ibn Moaaz."

Albara' reported that a garment of silk was presented to God's Messenger (PBUH). His Companions touched it and admired its softness; thereupon he said: "Do you admire the softness of this (cloth)? The handkerchiefs of Saad ibn Moaz in Paradise are better than this."

It was narrated by Ibn 'Umar that the Messenger of God said: "This is the one at whose death the Throne shook, the gates of heaven were opened and seventy thousand angles attended his funeral. He was talking about Saad ibn Moaz.

- Abdullah ibn Sahl ibn Zaid ibn 'Amer ibn Amr ibn Jasm

He is the brother of Rafi' ibn Sahl. He fought at Badr, Uhud, and the Trench where he was killed then.

- Amra bint Masud

She died in Medina while the Prophet (PBUH) and her son Saad ibn Ubada were at Dumat Aljandal

Ibn Abbas narrated: "The mother of Saad ibn Ubada died in his absence. He said, "O God's Messenger (PBUH)! My mother died in my absence; will it be of any benefit for her if I give Sadaqa on her behalf?" The Prophet (PBUH) said, "Yes," Saad said, "I make you a witness that I gave my garden called Al Makhraf in charity on her behalf."

- Kaab ibn Malik ibn Qais ibn Malik

He fought at Badr, Uhud and the Trench and he was killed then.

Then, the 6th Hijri year

Events:

Expedition of The Prophet (PBUH) through ibn Maslamah

A platoon of thirty Muslims under the leadership of The Prophet (PBUH) was dispatched for a military mission. It headed for the habitation of Banu Bakr. The Muslims attacked that tribe and dispersed them in all directions. Plenty of spoils were captured and the Muslims returned with the chief of the tribe of Banu Hanifa, called Thumamah ibn Uthal Alhanafi. During this raid the Muslims killed ten people while others fled with no resistance. The Muslims captured 150 camels and 3000 goats as booty. It took place in Muhharam.

Invasion of Banu Lahyan

It took place in Rabi' I. The Prophet (PBUH) wanted to get justice for the killing 10 Muslims in Expedition of Al Raji. Banu Lahyan was situated deep in the heart of Hijaz on the borders of Mecca, and due to deep-seated blood-revenge between the Muslims on the one hand, and Quraysh and the Arabians on the other hand.

The Prophet (PBUH) set out in Rabi' I with 200 Muslim fighters and made a trick of heading for Syria, then soon changed route towards tribe of Gharran, the scene of where 10 Muslims were killed in the Expedition of Alraji'. Banu Lahyan were on alert and got the news of his march, the tribe then immediately fled to the mountain tops nearby and thus remained out of his reach. On his way back, The Prophet (PBUH) dispatched a group of ten horsemen to a place called Kura' Alghamim, in the vicinity of Quraysh in order to indirectly confirm his growing military power. All these battles lasted for 14 days, after which he left back for home.

During this battle he (PBUH) passed by the grave of his mother

It is narrated that the Prophet (PBUH) while he was passing by Asafan, he found the grave of his mother Aminah bint Wahb, he performed ablution and prayed two rak'as, then he left.

Muslims asked him (PBUH) about what he did, he answered them that he passed by his mother's grave.

Then, there was Expedition of Ghaba

It is also known with Expedition of Dhu Qarad.

A few days after The Prophet (PBUH) returned to Medina from the raid on the Banu Lahyan, a band of armed men of Ghatafan led by Abdulrahman Uyanah ibn Hisn Alfazari invaded the outskirts of the city; and seized 20 camels. They also killed the shepherd and took his wife as a captive.

Abdulrahman Uyanah ibn Hisn Alfazari made a raid, looted the camels, and killed the shepherd and captured his wife. Salamah ibn Alakwa was the first to find this out.

The Prophet (PBUH) entitled Abdullah ibn Maktoum to manage the affairs of Medina and left Saad ibn Ubada together with 300 men to guard Medina.

The place by which it was fought is known as Dhu Qarad, a reservoir of water, at a day's journey from Medina. This incident took place three days before the battle of Khaibar.

A search for the camel and the kidnapped women was done, and they were brought back. The Prophet (PBUH) on his way back to Medina stopped at a place called Dhu Qarad and sacrificed a camel.

The Prophet (PBUH) collected 500-700 fighters, but followed up by sending 8 horsemen. Only 40 enemy horsemen were involved, and the booty captured by Muslims was 10 camels. Half the camels were recovered, and while doing so, the Muslims killed 4 of the raiders while suffering the loss of their own men. The Prophet returned to Medina on Monday after 5 days of absence.

Then, Expedition of Ukasha ibn Almihsan to Alghamir

Alghamir is a well that inhabited by Banu Asad in the year of six Hijri.

Upon an order by The Prophet (PBUH), a detachment of 30 Muslim fighters led by Ukasha ibn Almihsan was sent to the place of the enemy, that immediately fled leaving behind them 200 camels which were taken to Medina.

Then, there was the detachment of The Prophet (PBUH) through ibn Maslamah to Dhu Alqassah

It took place in Rabi' II

The Prophet (PBUH) sent a big herd of camels out to graze in the vicinity of Hayfa, which is seven miles from Medina, it was rich of green pastures. Owing to the incessant drought, Banu Thalabah, a section of the Ghatafan tribe, was tempted to steal from The Prophet (PBUH)'s herd.

Banu Thalabah tribe was already aware of the imminent attack; so they wait for the Muslims, and when The Prophet (PBUH) arrived at the site, Banu Thalabah, with 100 men trapped them, while the Muslims were making preparation to sleep; and after a brief resistance killed all of ibn Maslama's men. Ibn Maslama pretended to be dead. A Muslim who happened to pass that way found him and assisted him to return to Medina. The raid was unsuccessful.

Then, Detachment of Abu Ubaidah ibn Aljarrah to Dhu Alqassah

The first raid on Banu Thalabah was a failure, and many of The Prophet (PBUH)'s companions were trapped and killed. When the Prophet (PBUH) learned of this incident, he immediately dispatched an army of 40 soldiers under the leadership of Abu Ubaidah ibn Aljarrah in revenge for the killings of his companions. This army arrived there in Dhu Alqassah just before dawn. Immediately upon their arrival, they raided the inhabitants by surprise, but they quickly fled to the mountains. The Muslims took their cattle, clothes and captured one man. The captured man embraced Islam and the Prophet (PBUH) released him.

Then, Expedition of Zaid ibn Harithah to Banu Salim (Aljumum)

It occurred in Rabi' II.

A platoon, under the leadership of Zaid ibn Harithah, was sent to Al Jumum, the habitation of Banu Salim, in the same year. A group of Non-Muslims were captured. A woman from Banu Muzaina was also captured, and she showed them the way to the enemy's camp. There, the Muslims took some captives and gained a lot of booty. Later on, the Prophet (PBUH) granted the woman her freedom and married her to one of his followers.

Then, Expedition of Zaid ibn Harithah (Al'is)

It occurred in Jumada I. Zaid ibn Harithah, at the head of a 170 horsemen, set out to a place called Al'is, interrupted a caravan of Quraysh led by Abul 'As. Among the prisoners was Abul 'As, the son-in-law of the Prophet (PBUH), the husband of Zainab, The Prophet (PBUH)'s eldest daughter. In this expedition, the whole caravan was plundered, and a large store of silver was captured, some of those who guarded the Caravan were taken prisoner. Abu Al'as fled and took refuge in Zainab's house. He begged her to ask the Prophet (PBUH) for the restitution of his wealth. Abu

Al'as captors immediately agreed to release him from their captivity. Abu Al'as was greatly moved by this generosity; returned to Mecca, completed his affairs there, then returned to Medina and accepted Islam. He then rejoined his wife Zainab

Then, Third Raid on Banu Thalabah (Altaraf)

In Jumada II, it is narrated that The Prophet (PBUH) sent Zaid to Altaraf as the commander of 15 men to raid Banu Thaalabah and captured 20 of their camels but the tribe members had fled. He spent four days there and then returned to Medina.

Then, Expedition of Zaid ibn Harithah

When Dihyah ibn Khalifah Alkalbi, who was leaving Caesar, the Byzantine king, to whom he was sent by the Messenger of God (PBUH) with some of his merchandise. Alhunayd ibn 'Arid and his son 'Arid ibn Alhunayd Aldulay`i, a clan of Judham, attacked him and seized everything that he had. Such news reached some people of the Banu Dubayb, the kinsfolk of Rifa`ah who had embraced Islam. They responded and went after Alhunayd and his son.

When the news reached The Prophet (PBUH), he immediately dispatched Zaid ibn Haritha with 500 men to punish them. The attack led by Zaid ibn Harithah was a response to Dihyah ibn Khalifa Kalbi's call for help, after being attacked by robbers. The Muslim army fought and killed several of them, inflicting heavy casualties, including their chief, Alhunayd ibn Arid and his son, and captured 1000 camels, 5000 of their cattle, 100 women and boys. The new chief of Banu Judham who had embraced Islam appealed to The Prophet (PBUH) to release his fellow tribesmen, and The Prophet (PBUH) released them.

Then, Expedition of Abdulrahman ibn 'Awf

The Prophet (PBUH) appointed Abdulrahman ibn ‘Awf to head to Dumatul Jandal to win over the people and told Abdulrahman :

Fight everyone in the way of God and kill those who disbelieve in God. Do not be deceitful with spoils, do not be treacherous, nor mutilate, do not kill children. This is God’s ordinance and practice of his prophet among you.

Abdulrahman set out with 700 men on an expedition to Dumat Aljandal, that is on the route to Khaybar, Fadak. Following the Islamic rule, on reaching Dumat Aljandal, Abdulrahman called the people of the tribe to embrace Islam within three days.

During the 3 day-grace-period, Alasbagh, a Christian chief of Banu Kalb complied and many of his followers also embraced Islam. Other tribesmen also paid Jizya to Abdulrahman. On agreement to pay Jizya tax regularly, they were allowed to keep their Christianity. Abdulrahman married Tumadhir bint Alsbagh, the daughter of the Christian king and brought this lady with him to Medina.

Then, Expedition of Ali ibn Abu Talib (Fadak)

It is narrated that Ali ibn Abu Talib was dispatched as the commander of a detachment to the habitation of Banu Saad ibn Bakr in a place called Fadak. The Prophet (PBUH) had received some news that Banu Bakr had gathered to support the Jews of Khaybar.

The Muslim fighters used to march during the day and wait at night. On their way, they captured an enemy spy who admitted being sent to Khaibar tribe, to offer them support in return for their dates. Ali and his companions raided their camp, captured 500 camels and 2000 goats, but Banu Saad ibn Bakr tribe, with their chieftain Wabr ibn 'Aleem had fled away.

Then, Expedition of 'Abdullah ibn 'Atik to Abu Rafi' ibn Abu Huqaiq

It took place in Khaibar in the month of Ramadan

Sallam ibn Abu Huqayq (Abu Rafi') was Jewish, who aided and assisted the disbeliver enemies of the Muslims by provisioning them. A group of 5 men from the Banu Khazraj tribe with ‘Abdullah ibn ‘Ateeq at their head, moved to Khaybar where ‘Abu Rafi’s fort was situated. When they approached the fortress, 'Abdullah ibn 'Atik who was familiar with the language of the Banu Nadir, addressed Huqaiq's wife, who came to open the door, entering on a false pretext. When his wife saw they were armed, she began to cry and they started to direct their weapons at her, forcing her to be soundless. They then rushed in and killed Huqaiq.

On his way back, his leg broke so he enfolded it with a band, and hid in a secret place until morning when someone announced the death of Salam ibn Abu huqaiq officially. On hearing this news, he left and went to see The Prophet (PBUH), who listened to the whole story, and then asked ‘Abdullah to stretch his leg, which he wiped and the fracture healed on the spot.

Then, Expedition of Abdullah ibn Rawaha to Khaibar to kill Alyusair ibn Zaram

It took place in Shawwal. The assassination of Abu Rafi did not relieve The Prophet (PBUH) of his apprehensions. The Prophet (PBUH) did not feel safe from the Jews of Khaybar.

Alyusair ibn Zaram was elected the new chief of the Khaybar Jews. He maintained the same good relations with Banu Ghatafan that his predecessor Abu Rafi had. The Prophet (PBUH) heard that Alyusair ibn Zaram was planning a fresh attack against him. So he deputed Abdullah ibn Rawaha, a leader of Banu Khazraj, and sent him with three followers to Khaybar to gather intelligence on how Alyusair may be taken unaware and assassinated.

But Abdullah ibn Rawaha found the Jews to be very alert for this second assassination to be a success. When he returned to Medina a new strategy was put, the Prophet (PBUH) again sent him openly with 30 men mounted on camels to persuade Alyusair to visit Medina. When they arrived, they assured Alyusair they will make him the ruler of Khaibar and would treat him well, giving Alyusair ibn Zaram a sincere guarantee of his safety.

So he was mounted on the horse of Abdullah ibn Unais and the Muslims rode behind him. When they arrived at Qarqarat, about six miles from Khaybar, Alyusair distrusted the plans of the Muslims and changed his mind about going to meet the Prophet (PBUH). Then, he dismounted from the what he was riding with Abdullah ibn Unais. Abdullah ibn Unais perceived that Alyusair was pulling his sword. Thus, he rushed at him and hit him with a lethal blow. Alyusair fell wounded but hit Abdullah ibn Unais and wounded him with a camel staff, the only weapon he could reach. This was a signal for the Muslims to attack, each of the Muslims killed the Jews on the camels in front of them, one behind the other. The Muslims killed all the Jews, except one, who was able to escape.

Then, Expedition of Kurz ibn Jabir Al-Fihri in Shawwal

Eight members of Banu Uraynah, a Bedouin tribe, came to the Prophet (PBUH) and embraced Islam. They stayed in Medina but found its climate not suitable, so they were asked to pitch their tents in the pastures nearby, and were given water to drink. They then attacked the Prophet's shepherd Yasar, a freed slave, killed him and then drove off the camels.

Such news reached The Prophet (PBUH), who sent a group of twenty Muslims led by Karz ibn Jabir Alfihri on their track. The accused were brought back and handed over to the Prophet (PBUH). He had their hands and feet cut off and their eyes gouged out with hot iron, in recompense for their behavior, and then they were thrown on the stony ground till death.

It is narrated that Anas said: "Some people from 'Uraynah became Muslim, but the climate of Medina did not suit them. The Messenger of God (PBUH) said to them: 'Why don't you go out to some camels of ours and drink their milk?'- So they did that, and when they recovered they reverted to disbelief after their Islam, killed the herdsman of the Messenger of God (PBUH) , who was a believer, drove off the camels of the Messenger of God (PBUH), and fled as those at war. The Messenger of God (PBUH) sent someone to bring them and they were caught. He had their hands and feet cut off and their eyes branded, then he left them in Al-Harrah until they died."

Then, Mission of Amr ibn Umayyah Aldamri and Salama ibn Aslam to Abu Sufyan in Mecca

Amr ibn Umayyah Aldamri was sent on an task to kill Abu Sufyan (the leader of Quraysh), who had also sent a Bedouin to kill the Prophet (PBUH) .

The Prophet (PBUH) ordered the Mission of Amr ibn Umayyah Aldamri to kill Abu Sufyan to avenge Khubyab ibn Adi.

Quraysh ordered Khubyab ibn Adi to be crucified by Uqba ibn Alharith because he had killed Uqba ibn Alharith's father.

Amr ibn Umayyah Aldamri set out and first visited Kaaba where he was found by one of the Meccans. The Muslim assassins then fled and hid in a cave. While the Muslim's were still in the cave, Uthman ibn Malik Altamimi came close on his horse. Then Amr ibn Umayyah Aldamri came out and killed him, with a dagger he "stabbed him below the breast" and Altamimi gave out a loud scream which other Meccans heard.

The Muslims remained in the cave until the followers left. They then went to Altamimi and found the spot where Khubyab ibn Adi was crucified. They untied Khubayb from the cross, and traveled "forty paces" before they were spotted. He dropped Khubayb's body and again hid in a cave.

While he was in the cave, a Bedouin from Banu Bakr tribe passed by, he had only eye as he had lost the other. He asked "Who is there?", Aldamri replied: "One of Banu Bakr." The Bedouin laid down next to Aldamri and began to sing "I will not be a Muslim as long as I live." and Aldamri replied "You will soon see!" The Bedouin then went to sleep and Aldamri states:

I went to him and killed him in the most dreadful way. I leant over him, stuck the end of my bow into his good eye, and thrust it down until it came out of the back of his neck. After that I rushed out like a wild beast.

Aldamri then fled and came to a place called Alnaqi. At this place there were two Meccans sent as spies by Quraysh to check on the Prophet (PBUH). Aldamri "shot an arrow at one of them and killed him", and he then called on the other spy to surrender. After he surrendered, he tied him up, brought him to the Prophet (PBUH) and told him what happened after being questioned about it. The Prophet (PBUH) looked at him and laughed and said:

"Well done!" he said, and prayed for me to be blessed

In this year, Treaty of Hudaybiyyah

The Prophet (PBUH) had a presentiment that he entered Mecca and did circumambulation around the Kaaba. The Prophet (PBUH) and his companions all respected Mecca and Kaaba and they yearned to do circumambulation there. The Prophet (PBUH) together with his companions went out on the first day of Dhul Qi'dah 1st where he entitled Abdullah ibn Maktoum to manage the affairs of Medina. The Prophet (PBUH) and a group of 1,400 Muslims paraded unarmed towards Mecca, trying to perform the pilgrimage. They were dressed as pilgrims, and brought animals to sacrifice, hoping that Quraysh would honor the Arabian custom of allowing pilgrims to enter the city. The Muslims had left Medina in a state of ihram, a deliberate spiritual and physical state which controlled their freedom of action and banned fighting. This indicated that the pilgrimage was always intended to be peaceful.

The Prophet (PBUH) and his followers camp out of Mecca, and the Prophet (PBUH) met with Meccan representatives who wished to prevent the pilgrims' entry into Mecca.

Quraysh denied the Muslims entry into the city and located themselves outside Mecca, determined to offer confrontation even though the Muslims did not have any intention or preparation for battle. Muhammad camped outside Mecca at Hudaybiyyah and sent Uthman ibn Affan as an envoy to meet with the leaders of Quraysh and negotiate their entry into the city. Quraysh caused Uthman to stay longer in Mecca than they originally planned and refused to inform the Muslims of his location. This caused them to believe that Uthman had been killed by the people of Quraysh. On this occasion, Muhammad gathered his nearly 1,400 companions and called them to pledge to fight until death and take revenge for the death of Uthman. This pledge took place under a tree and was thus known as the Pledge of the Tree. During the same process, each companion came before Muhammad and pledged.

The Prophet (PBUH) came out in the year of Hudaibbiyyah with over ten hundreds of companions and when he came to Dhu al Hulaifah. He marked the animals of sacrifice. The Prophet moved on and when he came to the mountain, his riding-beast knelt down, and the people said twice: Go on, go on, Alqaswa has become tired. The Prophet (PBUH) said: She has not become tired, but He Who restrained the elephant has restrained her. He then urged her and she leaped up and stopped at the outermost side of Hudaibiyyah at a little-water pool. Meanwhile Budail ibn Warqa came and Urwah ibn Masoud joined him. He began to speak to the Prophet (PBUH). Whenever he spoke to the Prophet (PBUH), he caught his beard. Almughriah ibn Shubah was standing beside the Prophet (PBUH). He had a sword with him, wearing a helmet. Almughriah struck Urwah's hand with the lower end of his sheath, and said: Keep away your hand from his beard. Urwah then raised his hand and asked: Who is this? They replied: Almughirah ibn Shubah. He said: O treacherous one! Did I not use my offices in your treachery? In pre-Islamic days, Almughirah ibn Shubah accompanied some people and murdered them, and took their property. He then came (to the Prophet) and embraced Islam. The Prophet (PBUH) said: As for Islam we accepted it, but as to the property, as it has been taken by treachery, we have no need of it. He went on with the tradition the Prophet (PBUH) said: Write down: This is what Muhammad, the Messenger of God, has decided. He then narrated the tradition. Suhail then said: And that a man will not come to you from us, even if he follows your religion, without you sending him back to us. When he finished the document, the Prophet (PBUH) said to his Companions: Get up and sacrifice your animals and then shave.

The tree below which the pledge was carried out remained at its site until the second Rashidun Caliph, Umar, cut it down during his reign on the grounds that people had started attaching religious significance to it to the point of respect.

During the pledge, some inhabitants pounced dawn upon the Prophet (PBUH) and wanted to attack the Prophet (PBUH).

It has been narrated on the authority of Anas ibn Malik that eighty Persons from the people of Mecca pounced down upon the Messenger of God (PBUH) from the mountain of Tan'im. They were armed and wanted to attack the Prophet (PBUH). He captured them but spared their lives. So, God, the Exalted and Glorious, revealed the verses: "And it is He who withheld their hands from you and your hands from them within [the area of] Mecca after He caused you to overcome them. And ever is God of what you do, Seeing"." وَهُوَ الَّذِي كَفَّ أَيْدِيَهُمْ عَنكُمْ وَأَيْدِيَكُمْ عَنْهُم بِبَطْنِ مَكَّةَ مِن بَعْدِ أَنْ أَظْفَرَكُمْ عَلَيْهِمْ، وَكَانَ اللَّـهُ بِمَا تَعْمَلُونَ بَصِيرًا" (48:24).

In this year, the Plague was spread, it was the first plague.

In this year, Envoys sent to invite people to Islam in Dhul Hijjah

After signing the Hudaibiya treaty with Quraysh in Mecca, Muhammad sent several envoys in a few neighboring countries, inviting them to Islam. The following were sent:

Amr ibn Umayyah Aldamri to the king of Ethiopia (Abyssinia) called Aṣḥama ibn Abjar.

Dihyah ibn Khalifa Kalbi to the Byzantine king Heraclius.

Hatib ibn Abu Baltaeh to the king of Egypt called Muqawqis.

Alaa ibn Alhazermi to the king of Bahrain called Munzir ibn Sawa Al Tamimi.

Amr ibn Alaas to the king of Oman called Abd Aljalandi.

Salit ibn Amri to the king of Yamama called Hawza ibn Ali.

Shiya ibn Wahab to Haris ibn Ghasanni, the king of Damascus.

Abdullah ibn Hudhafah Assahmi to the emperor of Iran (Persia) called Khosrau II.

In this year, the Prophet used to use the seal.

Tale of what happened with those kings when they were sent envoys.

The Prophet sent Hatib ibn Abu Balta'ah to Muqawqis, ruler of Alexandria. He handed over to him the Prophet's letter and Muqawqis gave to the Prophet (PBUH) four Egyptian female servants as a gift common between rulers at that era, four of his own collection of slaves, one of whom was Mariah who then played a big role in the Prophet's life (PBUH) and became the mother of Ibrahim the Prophet's only son.

It is said that the delegation was sent in Dhul Hijja 6 A.H. Muqawqis sent his gifts to Muhammad in 7 A.H. Mariya bore Muhammad's son (Ibrahim).

Muqawqis ordered that the letter should be placed in an ivory chest, to be kept safely in the government treasury. Muhammad's letter to Muqawqis was eventually preserved in the Christian monastery of Akhmim in Egypt and he sent a letter for the Prophet but he did not convert to Islam.

Heraclius, the Ceaser, king of Byzantium

He dominated those from the Persians who invaded his land. One day, he dreamt a bad dream and waked up while he was distressed in that time, there was news about what occurred among the Arabs and the emergence of someone who claimed that he was a prophet. He asked that they had to get someone who could tell about what happened among them.

God's Messenger (PBUH) wrote to Caesar and invited him to embrace Islam and sent him his letter with Dihya Alkalbi whom God's Messenger (PBUH) ordered to hand it over to the Governor of Busra who would forward it to Caesar. Caesar as a sign of gratitude to God, had walked from Hims to Ilya (i.e. Jerusalem), when God had granted him victory over the Persian forces. Then, when the letter of God's Messenger (PBUH) reached him, he said after reading it, 'Seek for me any one of his people! (Arabs of Quraysh tribe) if present here, in order to ask him about God's Messenger (PBUH).

At that time Abu Sufyan ibn Harb was in the Levant with some men from Quraysh who had come to the Levant, as merchants during the treaty that had been concluded between the Messenger (PBUH); and the polytheists of Quraysh.

Abu Sufyan said "Caesar's messenger found us somewhere in the Levant so he took me and my companions to Ilya and we were admitted into Ceasar's court to find him sitting in his royal court putting on his head a crown and enclosed by the senior VIPs of the Byzantine. He said to his translator and assistant. 'Ask them who amongst them is a close relation to the man who claims to be a prophet." Abu Sufyan added, "I replied, 'I am the nearest relative to him.' He asked, 'What degree of relationship do you have with him?' I replied, 'He is my cousin.'

There was none of Bani Abu Manaf in the caravan except myself. Caesar said, 'Let him come nearer.' He then ordered that my companions stand behind me near my shoulder and said to his translator, 'Tell his companions that I am going to ask this man about the man who claims to be a prophet. If he tells a lie, they should contradict him immediately."

Abu Sufyan added, "By God! Had it not been shameful that my companions label me a liar, I would not have spoken the truth about him when he asked me. But I considered it shameful to be called a liar by my companions. So I told the truth. He then said to his translator, 'Ask him what kind of family does he belong to.' I replied, 'He belongs to a noble family amongst us.' He said, 'Have anybody else amongst you ever claimed the same before him? 'I replied, 'No.' He said, 'Had you ever blamed him for telling lies before he claimed what he claimed? 'I replied, 'No.' He said, 'Was anybody amongst his ancestors a king?' I replied, 'No.' He said, "Does the noble or the poor follow him?' I replied, 'It is the poor who follow him.' He said, 'Are they increasing or decreasing (day by day)?' I replied,' They are increasing.' He said, 'Does anybody amongst those who embrace his (the Prophet's) Religion become displeased and then discard his Religion?'. I replied, 'No.' He said, 'Does he break his promises? I replied, 'No, but we are now at truce with him and we are afraid that he may betray us."

Abu Sufyan added, "Other than the last sentence, I could not say anything against him. Caesar then asked, 'Have you ever had a war with him?' I replied, 'Yes.' He said, 'What was the outcome of your battles with him?' I replied, 'The result was unstable; sometimes he was victorious and sometimes we.' He said, 'What does he order you to do?' I said, 'He tells us to worship God alone, and not to worship others along with Him, and to leave all that our fore-fathers used to worship. He orders us to pray, give in charity, be chaste, keep promises and return what is entrusted to us.' When I had said that, Caesar said to his translator, 'Say to him: I ask you about his ancestry and your reply was that he belonged to a noble family. In fact, all the Prophets came from the noblest lineage of their nations. Then I questioned you whether anybody else amongst you had claimed such a thing, and your reply was negative. If the answer had been affirmative, I would have thought that this man was following a claim that had been said before him. When I asked you whether he was ever blamed for telling lies, your reply was negative, so I took it for granted that a person who did not tell a lie about the people could never tell a lie about God. Then I asked you whether any of his ancestors was a king. Your reply was negative, and if it had been affirmative, I would have thought that this man wanted to take back his ancestral kingdom. When I asked you whether the rich or the poor people followed him, you replied that it was the poor who followed him. In fact, such are the followers of the Prophets. Then I asked you whether his followers were increasing or decreasing. You replied that they were increasing. In fact, this is the result of true faith till it is complete in all respects. I asked you whether there was anybody who, after embracing his religion, became displeased and discarded his religion; your reply was negative. In fact, this is the sign of true faith, for when its cheerfulness enters and mixes in the hearts completely; nobody will be displeased with it. I asked you whether he had ever broken his promise. You replied in the negative. And such are the Prophet (PBUH) s; they never break their promises. When I asked you whether you fought with him and he fought with you, you replied that he did and that sometimes he was victorious and sometimes you. Indeed, they are put to trials and the final victory is always theirs. Then I asked you what he ordered you. You replied that he ordered you to worship God alone and not to worship others along with Him, to leave all that your fore-fathers used to worship, to offer prayers, to speak the truth, to be chaste, and to keep promises. These are really the qualities of a prophet who, I knew (from the previous Scriptures) would appear, but I did not know that he would be from amongst you. If what you say should be true, he will very soon occupy the earth under my feet, and if I knew that I would reach him definitely, I would go immediately to meet Him; and were I with him, then I would certainly wash his feet.'

"Abu Sufyan added, "Caesar then asked for the letter of God's Messenger (PBUH) and it was read. Its contents were: "In the name of God, the most Beneficent, the most Merciful (This letter is) from Muhammad, the slave of God, and His Prophet (PBUH), to Heraculius, the Ruler of the Byzantine. Peace be upon the followers of guidance. Now then, I invite you to Islam (i.e. surrender to God), embrace Islam and you will be safe; embrace Islam and God will bestow on you a double reward. But if you reject this invitation of Islam, you shall be responsible for misguiding the peasants (i.e. your nation). "Say, "O People of the Scripture, come to a word that is equitable between us and you - that we will not worship except God and not associate anything with Him and not take one another as lords instead of God." But if they turn away, then say, "Bear witness that we are Muslims [submitting to Him]"." "قُلْ يَا أَهْلَ الْكِتَابِ تَعَالَوْا إِلَىٰ كَلِمَةٍ سَوَاءٍ بَيْنَنَا وَبَيْنَكُمْ أَلَّا نَعْبُدَ إِلَّا اللَّـهَ وَلَا نُشْرِكَ بِهِ شَيْئًا وَلَا يَتَّخِذَ بَعْضُنَا بَعْضًا أَرْبَابًا مِّن دُونِ اللَّـهِ ، فَإِن تَوَلَّوْا فَقُولُوا اشْهَدُوا بِأَنَّا مُسْلِمُونَ" (3:64).

Abu Sufyan added, "When Heraclius had finished his speech, there was a great hue and cry caused by the Byzantine Royalties surrounding him, and there was so much noise that I did not understand what they said. So, we were turned out of the court.

It is said that Heraculius sent to one of the Jews and told them about the characteristics of the Prophet (PBUH) who told him that he was the last prophet, he was the prophet we was waiting. Heraculius gathered the Byzantines and told them that they realized that he was a prophet that his characteristics found in their Book, and encourage them to be under his rule, pay Jiziah and avoid wars against him but they refused.

Khosrow II, Khosrow Parviz was the last great Sasanian king (shah) of Iran.

Abdullah ibn Abbas narrated: God's Messenger (PBUH) sent his letter to Khosrow and ordered his messenger to hand it over to the Governor of Bahrain who was to hand it over to Khosrow. So, when Khosrow read the letter, he tore it. Said ibn Almusaiyab said, "The Prophet (PBUH) then invoked God to disperse, (destroy Khosrow and his followers severely)".

Khosrow II was a Persian king to whom Muhammad had sent a messenger, Abdullah ibn Hudhafah Assahmi, along with a letter in which Khosrow was asked to convert to the religion of Islam.

"In the name of God, the Beneficent, the Merciful.

From Muhammad, the Messenger of God, to Kisra, the great (leader/ head) of the Persians. Peace be upon him, who seeks truth and expresses belief in God and in His Prophet and testifies that there is no deity but God and that He has no partner, and who believes that Muhammad is His servant and Prophet. Under the Command of God, I invite you to worship Him. He has sent me for the guidance of all people so that I may avoid them his entire wrath. Embrace Islam so that you may remain safe in this life and the hereafter. And if you refuse to accept Islam, you will be responsible for the sins of the Magi.

Khosrow II tore up Muhammed's letter saying, "A pitiful slave among my subjects dares to write his name before mine" and commanded Badhan, his vassal ruler of Yemen, to dispatch two valiant men to identify, seize and bring Muhammad from Hijaz to him. When Abdullah ibn Hudhafah Assahmi told Muhammad how Khosrow had torn his letter into pieces, Muhammad promised the destruction of Khosrow II stating, "Even so, God shall destroy his kingdom."

Khosrow wrote to Badhan to sent two men from to seize the Prophet and send him to Khosrow. Badhan sent them who went to the Prophet. He told them to return to him on the following day.

News came from the heaven that God let Sheroe to kill his father. The two men returned to Badhan and told him about what the Prophet told. Badhan wondered and waited to check these news, after a short time, there was a message came from Sheroe who told him that he killed his father for the sake of the nobles of Persia and told him to let the man that Khosrow asked him to bring till further notice.

Khosrow II (Purviz) was the son of Hormizd IV and the grandson of Khosrow I. Khosrow II was the last king of Persia to have a lengthy reign before the Muslim conquest of Iran, which began five years after his death. He lost his throne, then, recovered it with Roman help. Ten years later, he went on to revenge from the Achaemenids, conquering the rich Roman provinces of the Middle East; much of his reign was spent in wars with the Byzantine Empire and struggling against tyrants such as Bahram Choibn and Vistahm.

During the Byzantine–Sasanian War (602–628), Khosrow expanded deep into western Asia Minor, besieging the Byzantine capital of Constantinople in 626. After the failure of such siege, Heraclius lanuched a counteroffensive, ruining all territorial gains by Khosrow II in the Levant, most of which were Anatolia, the western Caucasus, and Egypt. He then marched into the Sassanian capital of Ctesiphon. The Byzantines also regained the True Cross, which Khosrow had captured following his conquest of the Levant during the 602–628 war.

Hormizd IV had his prominent general Bahram Chob discredited and then discharged. Bahram, enraged by Hormizd's actions, responded in insurrection, and due to his noble status and his long military experience, his soldiers and many others joined him, as he fought Khosrow's men, who were heavily outnumbered, but managed to hold Bahram's men back in several clashes. However, Khosrow's men eventually began losing their morale, and were in the end defeated by Bahram's forces. He then appointed a new governor for Khorasan. Hormizd shortly had Vinduyih imprisoned, while Vistahm was able to scape from the court. Shortly, a coup under the two brothers occurred in Ctesiphon. The two brothers shortly had Hormizd killed. However, Bahram continued his march to Ctesiphon, with the pretext of claiming to avenge Hormizd. Bahram, however, ignored his warning.

Khosrow II moved to Constantia and prepared to attack Bahram's territories in Mesopotamia, while Vistahm and Vinduyih were mobilizing an army in Adurbadagan under the supervision of the Byzantine commander John Mystacon, who was also mobilizing an army in Armenia. Then and after a while, Khosrow, along with Comentiolus, the Byzantine commander of the south, invaded Mesopotamia. During this invasion, Nisibis and Martyropolis quickly decamped to them, and Bahram's commander Zatsparham was defeated and killed.

Bryzacius, One of Bahram's other commanders, was captured in Mosil and had his nose and ears cut off, and was afterwards sent to Khosrow II, where he was killed. Moreover, Khosrow II and the Byzantine general Narses then penetrated deeper into Bahram's territory, seizing Dara and then Mardin, where Khosrow was re-proclaimed king. Khosrow II, however, could not feel safe as long as Bahram was alive, and succeeded in having him murdered.

Vistahm sent a letter to Khosrow announcing his claim to the throne through his Parthian (Arsacid) heritage. Khosrow sent several armies against his uncle, but failed to achieve a decisive result. In conclusion, Khosrow called upon the services of the Armenian Smbat Bagratuni, who engaged Vistahm near Qumis. During the battle, Vistahm was murdered by Pariowk.

After the capture of Dastagird, the son of Khosrow, Sheroe, was released by the families of the Sasanian Empire. Sheroe, with Aspad Gushnasp leading his army, seized Ctesiphon and imprisoned Khosrow II. Sheroe, who had now assumed the dynastic name of Kavad II, then ordered Aspad Gushnasp to lead the charge of accusations against the deposed shah. Yet, Khosrow dismissed all accusations one by one and aristocrats of Persia enforced Sheroe to kill his father as it was not right to have two kings, so he killed his father Khosrow II.

Due to Kavad's actions, his reign is seen as a turning point in the Sasanian history, and has been argued by some scholars as playing a key role in the fall of the Sasanian Empire.

Khosrow's rule lasted for 38 years. When Sheroe assumed the rule, he lived in distress till he died 7 months later.

Regarding the king of Ethiopia

Letter of the Prophet to Armah, the Negus:

In the name of God, the most beneficial the Merciful. From Mohammed, the Prophet of Islam, to Nagaci king of Abyssinia:

Peace to you, there is no deity but God, the King, the Holy peace insured dominant. I invite you and your soldiers to God Almighty…..

Nagaci king of Abyssinia sent a message to the Prophet (PBUH) stating that he witnessed that he was the messenger of

God and he testified that what the Prophet was saying was true and from God.

It is narrated that the Prophet (PBUH) sent Shuja ibn Wahb Alasadi to Alharith ibn Abo Shamir Gassani to invite him to convert to Islam. He gave him the message that he threw on the ground after he read it asking who can seize my dominance and rule?

After the Hudaybiyyah Treaty, Muhammad sent a letter to Harith Gassani which read as follows:

From Muhammad, the Messenger of God to Alharith ibn Abo Shamir: Who follows true guidance and believes in it and regards it as true. I invite you to believe in One God with no associates, and your kingdom shall remain yours.

He wrote a message to Caesar telling him about this tale, Caesar sent to him a message that he did nothing and to go to him in Ilya'. He gave Shuja gold and clothing and asked him to salute the Prophet (PBUH) saying Peace be upon him. Alharith ibn Abo Shamir died in the year of Conquer of Mecca.

Hawdha ibn Ali Alhanafi

It is said that the Prophet (PBUH) sent Salit ibn Amr Alameri to Hawdha ibn Ali Alhanafi to invite him to Islam but he did not convert to Islam. He gave Salit a prize. He died before the Conquer of Mecca.

In this year, the land was dry and the Prophet (PBUH) performed the Rain-invoking prayer.

Tale of those who died in this year from the nobles

- Umm Ruman Zaynab bint Amir ibn Uwaymir Al-Kinaniyah

She married Alharith ibn Sakhbarah, who was from the Azd tribe, and they had one son, Tufayl. Shortly Umm Ruman was widowed and left unsupported. Abu Bakr then married her. They had two children: Abd Alrahman and Aisha. Umm Ruman migrated to Medina accompanied by Aisha and by her stepchildren Asma and Abdullah. Umm Ruman died in Medina.

It is narrated that while she was being put into her grave, Muhammad said, "Anyone who wants to know what a houri looks like should look at Umm Ruman."

- Utbah ibn Usaid ibn Jaber, Abu Basir:

He was an ally to Banu Zuhra. He converted to Islam in Mecca where he was prevented to migrate. At the time of Hudaybiyyah (treaty), he managed to flee from Mecca and went to the Prophet (PBUH) but it was stipulated that the Prophet (PBUH) should return to Quraysh whomever comes to him therefrom, even if he embraced his religion. When the Prophet (PBUH) returned to Medina, Abu Basir, the new Muslim came to him. The Infidels sent envoys in his pursuit who said (to the Prophet (PBUH)), "Abode by the promise you gave us." So, the Prophet (PBUH) handed him over to them. They took him out (of the City) till they reached Dhul-Hulaifa where they dismounted to eat some dates they had with them. Abu Basir said to one of them, "By God, O so-and-so, I see you have a fine sword." The other drew it out (of the scabbard) and said, "By God, it is very fine and I have tried it many times." Abu Basir said, "Let me have a look at it." When the other gave it to him, he hit him with it till death, and his companion ran away till he reached Medina and entered the Mosque running. When God's Messenger (PBUH) saw him he said, "This man appears to have been frightened." When he reached the Prophet (PBUH) he said, "My companion has been murdered and I would have been murdered too." Abu Basir came and said, "O God's Messenger (PBUH), by God, God has made you fulfill your obligations by your returning me to the Infidels, but God has saved me from them." The Prophet (PBUH) said, "Woe to his mother! What excellent war kindler he would be, should he only have supporters." When Abu Basir heard that he understood that the Prophet (PBUH) would return him to them again, so he went till he reached the seashore. Abu Jandal ibn Suhail got himself unconfined from the infidels and joined Abu Basir. So, whenever a man from Quraysh embraced Islam he would follow Abu Basir till they formed a strong group.

Whenever they heard about a caravan of Quraysh heading towards the Levant, they stopped it, attacked and killed the infidels and took their properties. Quraysh sent a message to the Prophet (PBUH) requesting him to send for (i.e. Abu Basir and his companions) promising that whoever came to the Prophet (PBUH) would be secure. The Prophet (PBUH) wrote to Abu Basir to come together with his companions to the Prophet. Upon the arrival of the message, he was passing away. His companions buried him then they went to the Prophet (PBUH).

Then, there was the 7th year of his migration (PBUH)

Events: Battle of Khaybar

It occurred in Jumada I. Khaybar is an oasis, which was located 150 kilometers from Medina in the north-western part of the Arabian peninsula.

The Prophet (PBUH) ordered to call for preparation for Battle of Khaybar. He (PBUH) deputed Seba ibn Arfattah to be responsible for Medina. He took Umm Salama, his wife, with him.

Anas ibn Mali narrated: God's Messenger reached Khaibar in the early morning and the people of Khaybar came out with their spades, and when they saw the Prophet they said, "Muhammad and his army!" and returned quickly to take refuge in the fort. The Prophet raised his hands and said, "God is Greater! Khaybar is ruined! If we approach a nation, then miserable is the morning of those who are warned."

He (PBUH) preached people and distributed banners; one for Ali ibn Abu Talib, a second one for Habab ibn Mundhir and the third one was for Saad ibn Ubada.

There was a severe fighting among the two parties and there were killed persons till The Prophet (PBUH) and his companions managed to conquer each fort of their forts.

As war with Muhammad seemed looming, the Jews of Khaybar entered into an alliance with the Jews of Fadak oasis. They also successfully persuaded the Bedouin Ghatafan tribe to join their side in the war in exchange for half of their products. However, in comparison to the power of the North, Muhammad's army did not seem to pose enough of a threat for Khaybar to adequately prepare themselves for the upcoming battle. Along with the knowledge that Muhammad's army was small, and in need of resources, the lack of central authority at Khaybar prevented any integrated defensive preparations, and quarrels between different families left the Jews confused. Banu Fazara, related to Ghatafan, also offered their assistance to Khaybar, after their unsuccessful negotiations with the Muslims.

After the forts at Annatat and those at Ashshiqq were captured, there remained the last and the heavily secured fortress called Alqamus, the siege of which lasted between thirteen and nineteen days.

It is reported that the strength of Muslims army ranged from 1,400 to 1,800 men and from 100 to 200 horses.

Among the captives was Safiyya bint Huyayy, daughter of the killed Banu Nadir chief Huyayy ibn Akhtab and widow of Kenana ibn Alrabi. The companions informed Muhammad of Safiyya's good family status, and requested him to accept her as his wife so as to reserve her prestige and status. Thus, Muhammad so accepted, freed and married her. Then, Safiyya became one of the Mother of the Believers.

The Jews of Khaybar were to evacuate the area, and surrender their wealth. The Muslims would cease the war and not hurt any of the Jews. After the agreement, some Jews asked Muhammad to continue to cultivate their orchards and remain in the oasis. In return, they would give one-half of their produce to the Muslims.

It is narrated: "When Ali reached the Citadel of Qamus, he met, at the gate, Marhab, a Jewish chief who was well experienced in battle. Marhab called out: Khaibar knows certainly that I am Marhab, A fully armed and well-tried valorous warrior (hero), when war comes spreading its flames.

'Ali chanted in reply: I am the one whose mother named him Haidar (lion), (And am) like a lion of the forest with a terror-striking countenance. I give my opponents the measure of sandara in exchange for sa' (goblet) (i.e. return their attack with one that is much more fierce).

The two soldiers struck at each other, and after the second blow, Ali cleaved through Marhab's helmet, splitting his skull and landing his sword in his opponent's teeth. Another narration described, "Ali struck at the head of Mirhab and killed him".

Muslims attempted in vain, to capture this fort. The first attempt was made by Abu Bakr who took the banner and fought, but was unable to succeed. Umar, then charged ahead and fought more forcefully than Abu Bakr, but again failed. That night Muhammad proclaimed, "By God, tomorrow I shall give the banner to a man who loves God and His Messenger, whom God and His Messenger love. God will bestow victory upon him." That morning, Quraysh were wondering who should have the honor to carry the banner, but Muhammad called out for Ali ibn Abu Ṭalib. The Prophet (PBUH) sent him with his flag and Ali, with new vigor, set out to meet the enemy, holding the banner of Muhammad

Anas (May God be pleased with him) reported: "There fell to the lot of Dihya a beautiful girl, and God's Messenger (PBUH) got her in exchange of seven heads, and then entrusted her to Umm Sulaim so that she might embellish her and prepare her (for marriage) with him. He (the narrator) said: He had been under the impression that she might spend her widowing period in her (Umm Sulaim's) house. (The woman) was Safiyya daughter of Huyayy. God's Messenger (PBUH) arranged the wedding feast consisting of dates, cheese, and refined butter. And the people ate to their fill.

A Jewish woman, Zeynab bint Alharith, attempted to poison Muhammad to avenge her killed relatives. She poisoned a piece of lamb that she cooked for Muhammad and his companions, putting the most poison into Muhammad's preferred part, the shoulder. This murder attempt failed because Muhammad recognised that the lamb was poisoned and spat it out, but one companion ate the meat and died.

Battle of Wadi Alqura

When the prophet (PBUH) set off from Khaybar, he went to Wadi Alqura.

Some scholars considered it within the Battle of Khaybar as the Prophet (PBUH) did not return to Medina. It is said that there was an arrow who killed the servant of the Prophet (PBUH).

Abu Huraira reported that when the Messenger of God (PBUH) returned from the expedition to Khaibar, he travelled one night, and stopped for rest when he became sleepy. He told Bilal to remain on guard during the night and Bilal prayed as much as he could, while the Messenger of Go) and his Companions slept. When the time for dawn approached Bilal leaned against his camel facing the direction from which the dawn would appear but he fell asleep while he was leaning against his camel, and neither the Messenger of God nor Bilal, nor anyone else among his

Companions got up, till the sun shone on them. God's Messengerwas the first of them to awake and, being alarmed, he called to Bilal who said:

Messenger of God, may my father and mother be offered as ransom for thee, which overpowered me overpowered you. He (the Holy Prophet, then) said: Lead the beasts on: so they led their camels to some distance. The Messenger of God (PBUH) then performed ablution and gave orders to Bilal who pronounced the Iqama and then led them in the morning prayer. When he finished the prayer he said: When anyone forgets the prayer, he should observe it when he remembers it, for God has said: "And establish prayer for My remembrance"." "وَأَقِمِ الصَّلَاةَ لِذِكْرِي" (20:14).

Also, The Prophet (PBUH) sent a message to Al Najashi to marry Umm Habiba to him (PBUH) and to send his companions who migrated to Abyssinia and they arrived during the distribution of the booty of Khaybar and the Prophet commended to have shares from the booty.

In this year Hatib ibn Abo Baltaah came back from Almuqawqis bringing Maria and her sister Sirin, his female mule Duldul, his donkey Ya'fur, and sets of garments. Hatib had invited them to become Muslims before he arrived with them, and Maria and her sister did so. The Messenger of God (PBUH) lodged them with Umm Sulaym bint Milhan. Maria was beautiful. The prophet sent her sister Sirin to Hassan ibn Thabit and she bore him Abdulrahman ibn Hassan.

Expedition of Umar ibn Alkhatab to Turbah

The expedition was led by Umar, at the order of the Prophet (PBUH), together with 30 men gainst a branch of the tribes of Hawazin at Turbah, a distance of 4 nights march from Medina. Turbah was on the way to Sana' and Najjran. Umar's troop travelled by night and hid by day. By the time the Muslim army arrived at the habitation, Hawazin already got news of the Muslim attack and they fled for their lives.

Expedition of Abu Bakr to Nejd

The prophet (PBUH) sent Abu Bakr leading a large platoon to Fazarah in Nejd. Many were killed and taken as prisoners.

Salamah said "We went out (on an expedition) with Abu Bakr. The Mesenger of God (PBUH) appointed him commander over us. We attacked Fazarah. I then saw a group of people which contained children and women. I shot an arrow towards them, but it fell between them and the mountain. They stood; I brought them to Abu Bakr. There was among them a woman of Fazarah. She wore a skin over her and she was accompanying her daughter who was the most beautiful of the Arabs. Abu Bakr gave her daughter to me as a reward. I came back to Medina. The Apostle of God (PBUH) met me and said to me "Give me the woman, Salamah. I said to him, I swear by God, she is to my liking and I have not yet untied he garment. He kept silence, and when the next day came, the Messenger of God (PBUH) met me in the market and said to me “Give me the woman, Salamah, by God, your father. I said the Messenger of God, I have not yet untied her garment. I swear by God, she is now yours. He sent her to the people of Mecca who had (some Muslims) prisoners in their hands. They released them for this woman.

Expedition of Bashir ibn Saad Alansari (Fadak)

It took place in Shaaban, 7 AH. The Prophet (PBUH) sent Bashir ibn Saad Alansari together with 30 men headed to Fadak to confront the Banu Murrah. Bashir and his men killed a large number of the enemy and seized a lot of their camels and cattle, Bashir drove off the camels and flocks. On his way back, the enemy gathered up forces and overtook the Muslims at night. They showered Bashir and his men with arrows, and killed all the Muslims except Bashir. Bashir managed to escape back to Muhammad.

Expedition of Ghalib ibn Abdullah Allaithi (Mayfah)

The Prophet (PBUH) sent Ghalib ibn Abdullah Allaithi as the commander of 130 men to Mayfah on the confines of Nejd. He was sent to launch an attack against Banu Awal and Banu Thalabah in Ramadan 7 A.H. Muslims put many to death, and drove off their camels and flock.

Usama, one of the fighters killed a man, after he had pronounced the testimony of God's Singleness at the last moment just before killing him, to which incident the Prophet (PBUH) commented addressing his Companions: "Would you rip open his heart to discern whether he is truthful or a liar?"

Expedition of Bashir Ibn Saad Alansari (Yemen)

In Shawwal, the Prophet (PBUH) received news that a large group of polytheists from Gatafan gathered to raid the borders of Medina with Uyaynah ibn Hisn. Bashir ibn Saad Alansari marched towards Yemen, leading 300 Muslim fighters. Having heard about the advent of the Muslims, the polytheists fled away leaving behind them a large amount of booty, which was captured, along with 2 men who later embraced Islam upon arrival to Medina.

Delegation of Alasharah

It is narrated that there was a delegation from Alasharah to the Prophet (PBUH), they were 50 men accompanied by Abu Mossa Alashari. When they were about to reach Medina, they used to say "Tommorrow, we will meet the beloved men, Muhammad and his men." When they reached Medina, they found the prophet (PBUH) and his men were in Khaybar. Then, they sworn pledge to the Prophet (PBUH) and converted to Islam.

Aldawsi came to Medina

It is narrated that when Tufayl ibn Amr Aldawsi converted to Islam, he invited his people to Islam. He together with 70 or 80 men of his people came to Medina while the Prophet (PBUH) was out in Khaybar. They directed to the Prophet (PBUH) and returned with him to Medina.

'Umrat Alqada' was in Dhul Qi'da that fulfilled by the Prophet (PBUH) together with two thousand followers (Men and women) who had accompanied him to Mecca. They intended to go there after they had withdrawn the previous year, after wild negotiations with Quraysh out of intention to complete the "minor pilgrimage". The Prophet left Abu Zarr Alghaffari to manage the affairs of Medina. On that occasion, Quraysh committed themselves to empty Mecca, to avoid clash between disbelievers and Muslims.

Anas reported that the Prophet (PBUH) entered Mecca during 'Umrat Alqada' and 'Abdullah ibn Rawahah was walking in front of him reciting verses of poetry. "O tribes of disbelievers get out of his way - today we will strike you about its revelation; a strike that removes the heads from the shoulders - and makes the friend not concerned about his friend." 'Umar said to him: "O Ibn Rawahah! Before the Messenger of God (PBUH), and in the sanctuary of God you utter poetry?" the Messenger of God (PBUH) said: "Leave him O 'Umar! For it is quicker upon them than the raining arrow."

The Prophet (PBUH) commended Belal to call for the prayer from above Kaaba. They stayed at Mecca for three days and at noon of the fourth day Muslims were called to leave Mecca. The Prophet (PBUH) married to Maymunah bint Alharith in Sarif, ten kilometres from Mecca. She was the last wife of the Prophet (PBUH).

Expedition of ibn Abu Al'awja' to Banu Salim.

The Messenger of God (PBUH) sent ibn Abu Al'aja' Alsalami in fifty men to Banu Salim. When he went out, there was a spy for the people of Banu Salim who preceded him and warned them before he reached them to gather before their arrival. When he came to them, he found them prepared for him. He invited them to Islam but they refused. They launched arrows against each other. He was wounded and he returned to Medina at the first day of Safar in the 8th Hijri year.

Tale of those who died in this year

- Bishr ibn Albara' ibn Ma'rur ibn Sakhr

He converted to Islam together with his father during Aqaba, he was one of the archers who fought at Badr and he fought at Uhud, the Trench and Khaybar, he was with the Prophet during Treaty of Hudaybiyyah. He ate instead of the Prophet (PBUH) from the poisoned sheep so he died.

- Thuwaybah

She was the servant of Abu Lahab. However, she was freed by Abu Lahab when the Prophet (PBUH) migrated to Medina.

Thuwaybah became Muḥammad's first nurse, after his first three days with his mother. The Prophet (PBUH) was making a good relationship with her while he was in Mecca. She died in the 7th Hijri year while his return from Khaybar.

- Kavad II ibn Khosrow II

He was called Sheroe, he killed his father and brother then he died after he lived in distress.

- Alwalid ibn Alwalid ibn Almughirah ibn Amr Almakhzumi

He went out with his people at Badr while he was following their religion but he was captivated. Then he was redeemed by his brother Khalid and Hisham but when he went out from Mecca, he returned to the Prophet (PBUH) and converted to Islam and stayed at Medina till he died. He was asked by his brother that he could convert to Islam before he was redeemed, he said that he would not convert to Islam except after being redeemed so as to not be said that he converted to Islam for fear of redemption.

The Eighth Year After Hijrah (AH)

The events that took place in this year:

The Reign of Ardashir III, the son of Sheroe

He was seven years old when he ruled, because there was no one belonging to the House of the Kingdom who was qualified to this position. But Shahrbaraz (also known as Shariyar), who had participated in fighting Heraclius according to the orders of Parviz, degraded child Ardashir. So, he besieged him, deceiving some of his soldiers. Then, he killed Ardashir III and took his position. As a result, some people resented that he murdered Ardashir III. So, they allied with each other to kill Shahrbaraz.

The Reign of Boran, the daughter of King Khosrow Parviz (also known as Khosrow II)

She appointed Farrukh as the chief minister. Then, she attempted to bring stability by the implementation of justice, reconstruction of the infrastructure and lowering of taxes. She told people that neither stability of the countries could be achieved by the aggression of men nor victory could be achieved by their plots. Rather, it is achieved only by the support of God. Her reign continued for a year and four months.

The Reign of Jashne Sadeh

He ruled after Boran for less than one month. He was one of the cousins of Parviz.

The Reign of Azar Midokht, the second daughter of king Khosrow II

When she ruled, she said that she would follow the way of her father Khosrow. The king of Persia at that time was Farrukh

Hormizd. He proposed to marry her but she sent to him saying: "A queen cannot marry. However, visit me on the night of so and so". Then, she killed him when he came to her. When his son, Rostam, knew about the murder of his father, he went to her with a great army to revenge for his father and killed her. She ruled for six months only.

Then a man among the descendants of Ardashir I reigned. He ruled for some days then was killed. Afterwards, another one reigned and he was also killed.

The Reign of Yazdegerd, the son of Shariyar and the grandson of Khosrow Parviz

The soothsayers had said before to king Khosrow: "One of your future grandsons will destroy your reign. The sign which refers to him is that his body has a defect". So, Khosrow deprived his sons of women. Then, Shahriyar complained to Sherine – the woman who adopted Shahriyar – that he wanted to marry, otherwise he would kill himself. She sent her reply to him that she could not allow a woman to enter into the palace except for a one who was unattractive. He agreed upon that. Sherine sent to him a maid working as a cupper. It was claimed that this maid was a daughter of one of the nobles but when Sherine got angry at her, she made her work this job. Shahriyar married this lady. Then, she became pregnant with Yazdegerd. So, Sherine have her apprehended till she begot. Sherine did not announce the news of the baby for five years. Then, she found that Khosrow longed for children when he became old. Therefore, she said to him: “O King, will you be glad if you see a grandson for you even if he will bring an adversity?”. He said: “I do not mind”. So, she let Yazdegerd enter to Khosrow and said to him who he was. Khosrow loves the young boy ardently. But one day, he remembered what had been said by the soothsayers. So, he unclothed the boy and saw the defect accordingly. He outraged and wanted to hit him severely but Sherine appealed earnestly to him to not to kill him. And she said to him: “If the kinship is doomed to be destroyed, there is no way to repel it”. He replied to her: “This is the ominous boy whom the soothsayers have told me about. Get him out. I do not want to see him anymore". So, Sherine commanded the soldiers to take Yazdegerd to Sistan.

It was said that when Sheroe killed his brothers, Yazdegerd fled to Istakhr. Then, the latter reigned. And he was killed in the caliphate of Uthman ibn Affan (May God be pleased with him). Thus, the reign of the Persian came to an end.

Among the events happened in this year was the embracement of Islam by Amr ibn Al As, Khalid ibn Al Waleed and Uthman ibn Talha

They came to Medina in Safar. When Amr saw the prominence of the Prophet (PBUH), he went to Al Najashi. Thereupon, he saw Al Najashi calling the people to follow the Prophet (PBUH). So, he got out to go to the Prophet (PBUH) to embrace Islam. In his way, he met Khalid ibn Al Waleed intending that also. So, they became Muslims.

Among the events happened in this year was the Expedition of Ghalib ibn Abdullah Al Laithi to Banu Al Mulawwih at Al Kadid in Safar

Jundub ibn Makith Al Juhany said: "The Prophet (PBUH) sent a brigade headed by Ghalib ibn Abdullah Al Laithi and I was one of them. The Prophet ordered us to raid Banu Al Mulawwih. So, we did".

The Expedition of Ghalib ibn Abdullah Al Laithi to the injured companions of Bashir ibn Saad in Fadak

The Prophet (PBUH) had ordered Al Zubayr ibn Al Awwam to go to the injured companions of Bashir ibn Saad. But when Ghalib ibn Abdullah Al Laithi returned from Al Kadid, the Prophet sent him, instead of Al Zubayr, at the head of two hundred men including Usama ibn Zaid to Fadak.

The Expedition of Shujaa ibn Wahb to Banu Amer in Rabi I

Umar ibn Al Hakam said: "The Prophet (PBUH) sent Shujaa ibn Wahb at the head of twenty four men to some people belonging to the tribe of Hawazin. The period of the expedition was fifteen nights.

Among the events was the Expedition of Kaab ibn Umair Al Ghifari

Al Zuhari said: The Prophet (PBUH) dispatched Kaab ibn Umair Al Ghifari at the head of fifteen men to a location beyond Wadi Al Qura (a region in the Levant) in Rabi I. They found a crowd of people. So, they called them to embrace Islam but the people refused and showered the Muslims with arrows killing all of them except one who was seriously wounded but he managed to muster up his energy to turn back to the Prophet (PBUH) to tell him what had happened. So, the Prophet (PBUH) became upset as a result.

Among the events was making a pulpit (mimbar) for the Prophet (PBUH)

It was narrated by Al Tufail ibn Ubayy ibn Kaab that his father said: "The Prophet of God (PBUH) used to pray facing the trunk of a date palm tree when the mosque was still a hut, and he used to deliver the sermon leaning on that trunk. A man from among his companions said: 'Would you like us to make you something upon which you can stand on Fridays so that the people will be able to see you and hear your sermon?' He said: 'Yes'. So he made three steps for him, as a pulpit. When they put the pulpit in place, they put it in the place where it stands now. When the Prophet (PBUH) wanted to stand on the pulpit, he passed by the tree trunk from which he used to deliver the sermon, and when he went beyond the trunk, it moaned, split and cracked. The Prophet (PBUH) came down when he heard the voice of the trunk, and rubbed it with his hand until it fell silent. Then, he went back to the pulpit and when he prayed, he prayed facing it. When the mosque was knocked down (for renovation) and (the pillars, etc.) were changed, Ubayy ibn Kaab took that trunk and kept it in his house until it became very old and the termites consumed it and it became grains of dust".

The Expedition of Mu'tah in Balqa governorate, near Damascus, in Jumada I, in the eighth year AH.

Islamic historical scholars said: The Prophet (PBUH) sent Al Harith ibn Umair Al Azdi on an errand to carry a letter to the ruler of Busra. On his way, he was intercepted by Sharhabeel ibn Amr Al Ghassani. The latter killed Al Harith. The Prophet (PBUH) was shocked on hearing the news and ordered a large army of three thousand men to go to discipline the transgressors. The Prophet (PBUH) said: Zaid ibn Haritha was appointed to lead the army. Jaafar ibn Abu Talib would replace him if he was killed, and Abdullah ibn Rawaha would succeed Jaafar in case the latter fell. If ibn Rawaha was killed, the Muslims would recommend a man among them to lead the army. A white banner was raised and handed over to Zaid by the Prophet. The Prophet (PBUH) commanded the army to reach the scene of the murder of Al Harith and invite the people there to profess Islam. Should the latter respond positively, then no war would ensue, otherwise fighting them would be the only alternative left.

The Muslim army then marched and the enemies of Islam heard about the news of that. So, the latter prepared to battle the Muslims. Sharhabeel mobilized more than a hundred thousand troops. The Muslims encountered such huge army of polytheists. Zaid began to fight tenaciously, raising the white banner, till he was killed. Then, Jaafar ibn Abu Talib took the banner and fought till he was also killed. A Roman soldier struck and cut him into two parts. Then, Abdullah ibn Rawaha proceeded to hold up the banner and fought till he was killed. Then, the Muslims chose Khalid ibn Al Waleed as a leader. God made His Prophet (PBUH) see the battlefield. When Khalid took the banner, the Prophet (PBUH) said: "This is the time when the fight is raging hot". The Muslims defeated their enemies although the army of the latter was so huge, of two hundred thousand soldiers. Heraclius was at the head of one hundred thousand Romans, and one hundred thousand men of the Arab tribes of Lakhm, Judham, Bahraa and Bali joined him.

Among the events that happened in Jumada Al Akhir in the eighth year AH. was the Expedition of Amr ibn Al As to Dhat Al Salasil, beyond Wadi Al Qura. The distance between it and Medina was ten days on foot.

Islamic historical scholars said: A tribe of Banu Qudaah planned to attack Medina. When the Prophet (PBUH) knew that, he appointed Amr ibn Al As to lead an expedition, which was consisted of three hundred men and thirty horses, against them. When ibn Al As approached the enemies, he found them assembled in large numbers, so he sent a messenger back to the Prophet (PBUH) asking him for reinforcement. As a response, the Prophet (PBUH) sent to him two hundred men, who included Abu Bakr Al Siddiq (the righteous one) and Umar ibn Al Khattab, headed by Abu Ubaidah ibn Al Jarrah.

It was narrated by Amr ibn Al As:

I had a sexual dream on a cold night in the battle of Dhat Al Salasil (the battle of the Chains). I was afraid, if I washed I would die. I, therefore, performed tayammum (i.e. dry ablution) and led my companions in the Dawn prayer. When we returned, they mentioned that to the Prophet (PBUH). In turn, he said: 'O Amr, you led your companions in prayer while you were sexually defiled?'. I informed him of the cause which impeded me from washing. And I said: I heard God say: "And do not kill yourselves. Indeed, God is to you ever Merciful" "ولا تقتلوا أنفسكم إن الله كان بكم رحيمًا". (4:29). The Prophet (PBUH) laughed and did not say anything".

Among the events was the Expedition of Abu Ubaidah ibn Al Jarrah

In Rajab, the Prophet (PBUH) sent an expedition consisting of three hundred persons, including Umar ibn Al Khattab (May God be pleased with him) and appointed Abu Ubaidah ibn Al Jarrah as their leader, to the tribe of Juhaynah towards the seacoast, five nights journey from Medina. Jabir ibn Abdullah said that the expedition was sent for the purpose of looking out for a Quraysh caravan. The Muslim army run out of food and suffered from famine, so that they were obliged to eat leaves. That's why it was called the Expedition of Leaves. Then, they caught a large fish (sperm whale) that came ashore and ate it. There was no fighting.

Among the events was the Expedition of Abu Qatadah ibn Rabi Al Ansari to Khadirah in Najd in Shaaban

The Prophet (PBUH) sent Abu Qatadah at the head of fifteen men to Ghatafan. The expedition took fifteen nights and resulted in the murder of some polytheists and the capture of others in addition to confiscating large amounts of flocks.

Among the events was the Expedition of Abu Qatadah ibn Rabi Al Ansari to Batn Edam in Ramadan

When the Prophet (PBUH) planned to attack Mecca, he sent an expedition of eight men under the leadership of Abu Qatadah to Batn Edam, which lied at a short distance from Medina. That was for the purpose of diverting the attention of people from the main target of attacking Mecca as the people would think that the Prophet was among that expedition. A tribe, headed by Amer ibn Al Adbat, passed by the Muslims and Amer greeted them with their greeting (by saying peace be upon you). But Muhallam ibn Jaththamah, who was one of the Muslims in the expedition, killed him and confiscated the flock. Therefore, this verse of the Holy Qur'an has been revealed about those Muslims: "O you who have believed, when you go forth [to fight] in the cause of God, investigate; and do not say to one who gives you [a greeting of] peace "You are not a believer". " يا أيها الذين آمنوا إذا ضربتم في سبيل الله فتبينوا ولا تقولوا لمن ألقى إليكم السلام لست مؤمنًا" (4:94). They did not encounter a tribe to fight. So, they turned back. Thereupon, they were informed that the Prophet (PBUH) had directed to Mecca. Then, they met him at Al Suqya.

Among the events was the Conquest of Mecca in Ramadan

Islamic historical scholars said: After a period of twenty two months following the Treaty of Hudaybiyyah, the tribe of Banu Nafatha – belonging to Banu Bakr – sought the nobles of Quraysh to help them attack Banu Khuzaah. So, Quraysh agreed and provided them with weapons and men, without any concern for the truce – Treaty of Hudaybiyyah – held between them and the Prophet (PBUH). Then, twenty men of Banu Khuzaah were killed. Accordingly, Banu Khuzaah sought help from the Prophet (PBUH) and he promised he would advocate them. Then, Quraysh sent Abu Sufyan ibn Harb to the Prophet asking him to renew the treaty they had breached. But the Prophet (PBUH) refused and assembled a large army, keeping the objective of the operation secret. The Arab tribes in the regions surrounding the

Prophet (PBUH) embraced Islam and joined the Muslim army. So, the sum of the Muslim army was ten thousand soldiers.

The tribe of Quraysh was afraid that the Prophet (PBUH) might conquer them. So, they sent Abu Sufyan to bring them the news and take a promise of peace from Prophet Mohammed. When Abu Sufyan and two other men accompanying him saw the Muslim army, they got scared. Thereupon, Al Abbas ibn Abd Al Muttalib took Abu Sufyan and his two companions to the Prophet (PBUH) and they adopted Islam. As a result, the Prophet (PBUH) declared: “He who enters the house of Abu Sufyan will be safe, and he who closes his door will be safe”.

Then, the Prophet (PBUH) entered Mecca. So, people embraced Islam willingly or unwillingly. The Prophet (PBUH) performed Tawaf around the Kaaba. All of the idols that were around the Kaaba – a sum of three hundred and sixty idols – were destroyed by the appointing of the Prophet (PBUH) towards them, reciting the verse: “Truth has come, and falsehood has departed”. "جاء الحق وزهق الباطل" (17:81).

It was narrated that Ibn Abbas reported: The Prophet (PBUH) said on the day of the Conquest of Mecca: There is no more Hijrah (migration), but rather Jihad (striving in the cause of God) and good intention”.

It was narrated from Abu Huraira that the Prophet (PBUH) climbed Mount Al Safa on the day of the Conquest of Mecca and delivered an address. Then, Some of the Ansar (the helpers) whispered among themselves: "After all, love for his city and tenderness towards his relations have overpowered him". At that moment, the Divine revelation came to the Prophet (PBUH) with what the Ansar have said. So, the Prophet (PBUH) said: "O you assembly of the Ansar!". They said: "Here we are at your disposal, Prophet of God". He said: "You were saying that love for his city and tenderness towards his people have overpowered this man". They said: "So it was". He said: "No, never. I am a bondman of God and His Prophet. I migrated towards God and towards you. I will live with you and will die with you". So, they (the Ansar) turned towards him in tears. And they said to the Prophet: "We swear by God that we said so because of our tenacious attachment to God and His Prophet". The Prophet (PBUH) replied to them: "God and His Prophet testify you are truthful".

The Conquest of Mecca was on Friday, corresponded to 20 Ramadan. The Prophet (PBUH) stayed there for fifteen nights, then he went to Hunayn. He recommended Attab ibn Usayd to lead the people in Mecca in prayer. And he told Muadh ibn Jabal to teach them Sunnah and Islamic jurisprudence (Fiqh).

Among the events was the Expedition of Khalid ibn Al Waleed to destroy the idol called Al Uzza in 25 Ramadan

The Prophet (PBUH) sent Khalid ibn Al Waleed to destroy the idol of the goddess called Al Uzza, which was the greatest idol worshipped by the tribe of Quraysh and all of Banu Kinanah. Khalid went at the head of thirty men to do so, then he turned back to the Prophet (PBUH). The latter asked him if he had seen anything else there, to which Khalid replied, "No". The Prophet said to him that the idol had not been destroyed and commanded him to go back and fulfill the task. Khalid went again to the same place – named Nakhla – and there he saw a black woman, naked with disheveled hair. He struck her with his sword and cut her into "two pieces". He turned back and told that to the Prophet (PBUH). So, the Prophet said: “That is the real Al Uzza”.

The Expedition of Amr ibn Al As to destroy the idol of Suwaa in Ramadan

Upon the conquest of Mecca, the Prophet (PBUH) sent Amr ibn Al As to demolish the idol called Suwaa, which was worshipped by Banu Hudhail. On a question posed by the gatekeeper, Amr said he had been ordered by the Prophet (PBUH) to knock down the idol. The gatekeeper warned Amr that he would not be able to do it. Amr approached the idol and destroyed it. And he ordered his companions to break down its casket. Consequently, the gatekeeper embraced Islam.

Among the events was the Expedition of Saad ibn Zaid Al Ashhaly to Al Mashallal to destroy idol of Manat in Ramadan

Upon the conquest of Mecca, the Prophet (PBUH) sent Saad ibn Zaid Al Ashhaly, at the head of twenty men, to demolish the idol called Manat, worshipped by the polytheist tribes of Al Aws, Al Khazraj and Ghassan. There, a black woman appeared, naked with disheveled hair, wailing and beating on her chest. Saad immediately killed her and destroyed the idol.

Saad ibn Zaid had experienced the expeditions of Badr and Uhud and all of the battles with the Prophet (PBUH).

Among the events was the Expedition of Khalid ibn Al Waleed Al Makhzumi to Banu Jadhimah in Lower Mecca towards Yalamlam

Upon the return of Khalid ibn Al Waleed from the expedition to Nakhla to destroy Al Uzza, he was dispatched, by the Prophet (PBUH), at the head of three hundred and fifty men, to peacefully call Banu Jadhimah to embrace Islam. That was in Shawwal (the tenth month in the Islamic calendar). When Khalid reached them, they said to him that they embraced Islam. He ordered them to disarm. Then, he killed some of them because he sensed that their acknowledgment of embracing Islam was a trick. But when such news reached the Prophet (PBUH), he said: "O God, I disavow what Khalid has done". In addition, he sent Ali ibn Abu Talib (May God be pleased with him) to pay blood money to all those who had lost their people.

In this year, some considerable persons embraced Islam; Abu Sufyan ibn Al Harith, Abdulla ibn Abu Omayya ibn Al Mughira, Ah Harith ibn Hisham, Ikrimah ibn Abu Jahl, Hisham ibn Al

Aswad, Huwaitib ibn Abd Al Uzza, Shaibah ibn Uthman and An-Nadr ibn Al Harith.

Among the events was the Expedition of Hunayn, which is a valley far from Mecca by three nights, also called the Expedition of Hawazin

Upon the conquest of Mecca by the Prophet (PBUH), the tribe of Hawazin allied with the tribe of Thaqif against the Muslims. So, the Prophet (PBUH) encountered them, in Shawwal, with twenty thousand soldiers: Ten thousand Muslims out of them were belonging to Medina while the other two thousand Muslims were belonging to Mecca. The Muslims prided themselves on the large number of their soldiers and one of them said: "We shan't at all be defeated, because our army is huge today".

However, the army of Hawazin was so huge and started a fierce attack against the Muslims, who were compelled to retreat. Thus, God says: "God has already given you victory in many regions and [even] on the day of Hunayn, when your great number pleased you, but it did not avail you at all, and the earth was confining for you with its vastness; then you turned back, fleeing". " لقد نصركم الله في مواطن كثيرة ويوم حنين إذ أعجبتكم كثرتكم فلم تغن عنكم شيئًا وضاقت عليكم الأرض بما رحبت ثم وليتم مدبرين". (9:25). Then, the Prophet (PBUH) kept calling them: "O advocators of God and His Prophet, I am the slave of God and His Prophet". Then, the Muslims turned back to him. Among the ones who stayed behind and fought with the

Prophet were Ali ibn Abu Talib, Al Abbas, Al Fadl, Abu Sufyan ibn Al Harith ibn Abd Al Muttalib, Rabiaa ibn Al Harith, Abu Bakr Al Siddiq, Umar ibn Al Khattab and Usama ibn Zaid.

Then, the Prophet (PBUH) threw pebbles in the face of the enemy. Then, he said twice: "By the Lord of the Kaaba, they have been defeated".

Jabir ibn Abdullah reported: When the Prophet (PBUH) was distributing spoils of war (of the expedition of Hunayn) at Jirana, a man said to him: "O Mohammed, do justice". Upon this, Umar ibn Al Khattab said: "O Prophet of God, permit me to strike the neck of this hypocrite". However, the Prophet (PBUH) said: "This man and his companions recite the Qur'an but it does not go any deeper than their collarbones. They pass through Islam like an arrow passing through its target". That's why this verse of Holy Qur'an has been revealed about this man: "And among them are some who criticize you concerning the [distribution of] charities. If they are given from them, they approve; but if they are not given from them, at once they become angry". " ومنهم من يلمزك في الصدقات فإن أعطوا منها رضوا وإن لم يعطوا منها إذا هم يسخطون". (9:58). It was said that this man was called Dhul Khuwaysirah Al Tamimi.

Among the events was sending Al Alaa ibn Al Hadrami to Al Mundhir ibn Sawi at Al Bahrain, calling him to embrace Islam

When the Prophet (PBUH) left Jirana, he sent Al Alaa ibn Al Hadrami with a letter to Al Mundhir ibn Sawi Al Abdi at Al

Bahrain in order to call him to embrace Islam. Al Mundhir sent his reply to the Prophet (PBUH); announcing his conversion to Islam and telling him that some of his nation embraced Islam whereas others did not and asking for his consultation. So, the Prophet (PBUH) replied to him that jizyah (i.e. poll tax) would be levied on the Jews and Zoroastrians.

Among the events was the Expedition of Al Tufail ibn Amr Al Dawsi to destroy the idol of Dhul Kaffain (of the tribe of Daws)

When the Prophet (PBUH) wanted to conquer Al Taif, he sent Al Tufail ibn Amr to the tribe of Daus to destroy the idol of Dhul Kaffain worshipped by them. He also ordered Al Tufail to request the assistance of his tribe, then, to join him at Al Taif. So, Al Tufail demolishes the idol of Dhul Kaffain. Accordingly, four hundred men of his tribe went with him to advocate the Prophet (PBUH) in Al Taif. Then, the delegation of Banu Thaalabah came to the Prophet and he protected them.

Among the events occurred in Shawwal was the expedition of Al Taif

After the success of the expedition of Hunayn, the Prophet (PBUH) directed to Al Taif to conquer it. Its people were the tribe of Thaqif. They built a fortress and prepared for fighting. The Prophet (PBUH) camped near to their fortress. Then, Thaqif shot arrows at the Muslims and injured them. There, Abdullah ibn Abu Bakr Al Siddiq was killed. So, the Prophet (PBUH) besieged

Thaqif for fifteen days – and it was said that the siege lasted for forty days.

The embracement of Islam of Urwah ibn Masoud Al Thaqafi

God had guided him to Islam. So, he went to the Prophet (PBUH) to permit him to call his people to embrace Islam. The Prophet (PBUH) warned him that they would kill him but he insisted to do so and the Prophet permitted him. Then, when he called them to embrace Islam, they conspired against him. He was glad by his martyrdom.

Rising prices during the epoch of the Prophet (PBUH) occurred in this year

It was narrated by Anas ibn Malik that:

When prices rose during the time of the Prophet (PBUH), people said: “O Prophet of God , prices have shot up, so fix prices for us”. Thereupon, the Prophet (PBUH) said: “God is the one Who fixes prices, Who withholds, gives lavishly and provides, and I hope that when I meet God, none of you will have any claim on me for an injustice regarding blood or property”.

In Dhul Hijjah (the twelfth and final month in the Islamic calendar, the month of Pilgrimage) of this year was the birth of Abraham, the son of the Prophet (PBUH)

It was narrated from Abdullah ibn Abd Al Rahman ibn Abu Saasaa that: Maria bore the Prophet (PBUH) a son, Abraham (pronounced as Ibrahim). The Prophet sacrificed a sheep for his son a week after his birthhood. In addition, he had his son's hair cut and gave charity to the needy as much as the weight of his hair.

Tale of the nobles who died in this year

Jaafar ibn Abu Talib ibn Abd Al Muttalib ibn Hashim

He embraced Islam in its early times. Then, he migrated to Abyssinia – i.e. Al Habasha (in the second migration there), accompanying his wife Asmaa bint Umays (the daughter of Umays) who there gave birth to Abdullah, Mohammed and Awn. He stayed there till he went to the Prophet (PBUH) upon the conquest of Khaybar.

The Prophet (PBUH) had appointed Zaid as the leader of the Muslim army in the expedition of Mu'tah and he ordered that Jaafar ibn Abu Talib would replace him if he was killed. So, Jaafar fought until both his arms were cut off and he was eventually killed. The Prophet (PBUH) said that God made a pair of wings for Jaafar to fly with them in the Heaven in place of his two arms which were cut off.

Al Huwairith ibn Abdullah ibn Khalaf ibn Malik ibn Abdullah, nicknamed the Rejecter of Meat

He was nicknamed so, because he had refused to eat of the meats that were sacrificed to idols. He was killed when he was accompanying the Prophet (PBUH) in the expedition of Hunayn.

Zaid ibn Haritha ibn Sharahil ibn Abd Al Uzza ibn Imru' Al Qais

It was nicknamed Al Hibb, which means the beloved one to the Prophet. When his mother, Suda bint Thaalabah ibn Amer, visited her people with him, Banu Al Qayn made a raid there during the pre-Islamic period. And they sold Zaid at Souq Okadh (a famous market called Okadh). Hakeem ibn Haram purchased him for four hundred Dirham for his paternal aunt, Khadijah. In turn, she granted him to the Prophet (PBUH) when he married her.

When the father and uncle of Zaid went to the Prophet to take their son, the Prophet (PBUH) let the choice for Zaid. And the latter chose to stay with the Prophet. His father and uncle became astonished; how he preferred slavery (to be a slave to Mohammed) to freedom and his family. Zaid replied that he never saw a man of Mohammed's perfect character. Therefore, the Prophet (PBUH) pronounced that Zaid would be his son. And he was called Zaid ibn Mohammed till the time of Islam. Then, the Prophet (PBUH) married him to Zainab bint Jahsh. And when he divorced her, the Prophet (PBUH) married her. So, people said that the Prophet married the woman of his son. That's why this verse of the Holy Qur'an has been revealed: "Muhammad is not the father of [any] one of your men, but [he is] the Messenger of God and last of the prophets.". " ما كان محمد أبا أحد من رجالكم ولكن رسول الله وخاتم النبيين". (33:40). Also, God says in another verse: "Call them by [the names of] their fathers". "ادعوهم لآبائهم" (33:5). Consequently, he was called Zaid ibn Haritha from that day forth. It was said that all of this was reported from Mohammed ibn Saad.

Islam historical scholars said: "Zaid experienced the expeditions of Badr, Uhud, khandaq (Trench), Hudaybiyyah and Khaybar. When the Prophet went for the expedition of Al Muraysi, he appointed Zaid as a successor upon Medina. He was the only one, among the companions of the Prophet (PBUH), whose name is mentioned in the Holy Qur'an". Zaid was killed during the expedition of Mu'tah in Jumada I of the eighth year at the age of 52.

Zainab, the daughter of the Prophet (PBUH)

She was the elder daughter of the Prophet and the first one to marry among her sisters. She married the son of her maternal aunt, Abu Al As ibn Al Rabi. She gave birth to Ali and Umama. She embraced Islam and migrated with the Prophet (PBUH). She died in the beginning of the eighth year AH.

Suraqa ibn Amr ibn Atiya

He experienced the expeditions of Badr, Uhud, khandaq, Hudaybiyyah, Khaybar and Umrat Al Qadaa (The Compensatory Umrah). He was killed during the expedition of Mu'tah.

Shahrbaraz

He killed Ardashir III, the son of Sheroe, and became the king instead of him for forty days before being killed.

Abdullah ibn Rawaha ibn Thaalabah, nicknamed Abu Mohammed

He was one of the seventy men who experienced Al Aqaba. He was among the twelve selected leaders who gave the pledge of allegiance to the Prophet (PBUH). He experienced the expeditions of Badr, Uhud, khandaq, Hudaybiyyah, Khaybar and Umrat Al Qadaa. The Prophet headed him over Medina when he went for the expedition of Badr Al Mawid. He was martyred during the expedition of Mu'tah in the eighth year AH.

Ubadah ibn Qais ibn Absa, the uncle of Abu Al Dardaa

He experienced the expeditions of Badr, Uhud, khandaq, Hudaybiyyah and Khaybar. He was killed during the expedition of Mu'tah at the age of 40.

Abdullah ibn Zamaa ibn Al Aswad ibn Al Muttalib

He was one of the early Muslims in Mecca. He was one of those who migrated to Abyssinia (in the second migration there). And he was killed on the day of the expedition of Al Taif...

CHAPTER 7

The Ninth Year After Hijrah (AH)

Among the events that took place in this year:

The Expedition of Uyainah ibn Hisn against Banu Tamim in Muharram (the first month of the Islamic calendar)

The Prophet (PBUH) despatched Uyainah at the head of fifty horsemen to Banu Tamim. None of them was belonging to the Muhajireen (emigrants) or the Ansar. Uyainah attacked the tribe and captured 11 men, 11 woman and 30 boys and took them to Medina. Therefore, a few of the chiefs of Banu Tamim went there to free the captured. When they met each other, women and children cried. So, the chiefs hastened to the house of the Prophet (PBUH) and called him to get out to them. That's why this verse of the Holy Qur'an has been revealed for them: "Indeed, those who call you, [O Muhammad], from behind the chambers - most of them do not use reason". " إن الذين ينادونك من وراء الحجرات أكثرهم لا يعقلون" (49:4). Then, the Prophet gave them back the captured.

During this year, a large number of delegations came to the Prophet (PBUH) in Medina to announce their embracement of Islam

The coming of the delegation of Banu Fazara to the Prophet (PBUH)

It was said by Abu Wajza Al Saadi that: Upon the return of the Prophet (PBUH) from the expedition to Tabuk – which was in the ninth year AH – a delegation of Banu Fazara came to him to profess Islam. They complained to the Prophet (PBUH) that they suffered drought and asked him to supplicate his Lord for them.

So, the Prophet ascended the pulpit and supplicated: "O God! Provide water for Your servants and Your cattle, display Your mercy and give life to Your dead land. O God! Send wholesome, productive rain upon all of us, sooner rather than later, beneficial and not harmful". So, it rained heavily and they did not see the sun for six days. Then, the Prophet (PBUH) ascended the pulpit and supplicated: "O God! Let it rain around us and not upon us. Let it rain on the plateaus, hills and mountains, the bottoms of the valleys and places where the trees grow".

The coming of the delegation of Banu Tujib to the Prophet (PBUH)

It was narrated from Abu Al Huwairith that: The delegation of Banu Tujib came to the Prophet (PBUH) in the ninth year AH. They were thirteen men and gave the Prophet Zakah (charity) that God had imposed upon them to pay. Accordingly, the Prophet (PBUH) became pleased. He honored, greeted and gave them more than he gave to any other delegation.

The coming of the delegation of Banu Asad to the Prophet (PBUH)

When they came to the Prophet (PBUH), they said to him: We independently came professing Islam although you did not send a messenger to call us to embrace Islam. That's why this verse of the Holy Qur'an has been revealed about them: "They consider it a favor to you that they have accepted Islam". " يمنون عليك أن أسلموا" (49:17).

The coming of the delegation of Banu Kilab to the Prophet (PBUH)

When they came to the Prophet (PBUH), they said to him: Al Dahhak ibn Sufyan told us about the Holy Qur'an and Sunnah and called us to worship God, the Mighty and Sublime. We responded to God and His Prophet. And he collected Zakah from the wealthy among us and gave it to the poor among us.

The coming of the delegation of Baliy to the Prophet (PBUH)

They came to the Prophet (PBUH) in Rabi I. Ruwaifi ibn Thabit Al Balawi firstly received them.

The coming of the delegation of Urwah ibn Masoud Al Thaqafi to the Prophet (PBUH)

He embraced Islam.

The coming of the delegation of Al Taif to the Prophet (PBUH)

Abd ya Layl ibn Amr headed them. They embraced Islam in Ramadan.

The coming of the delegation of Bahraa to the Prophet (PBUH)

They were thirteen men who were received by Al Miqdad ibn Amr.

The coming of the delegation of Tayy and delegation of Saad ibn Huzaim to the Prophet (PBUH)

They were belonging to the people of Yemen.

The Prophet (PBUH) sent Al Waleed ibn Uqbah ibn Abu Muayt to Banu Al Mustaliq, a sub-clan of Banu Khuzaah, to collect Zakah from them

They had embraced Islam and built mosques. When they knew that Al Waleed ibn Uqbah approached them, they went out to receive and welcome him rejoicingly with sheep. When he saw them, he turned back to Medina, telling the Prophet (PBUH) that they pointed weapons at him. Consequently, the Prophet was about to send an expedition to fight them. So, upon knowing that, they came to the Prophet to tell him about the truth. Therefore, this verse of the Holy Qur'an has been revealed: "O you who have believed, if there comes to you a disobedient one with information, investigate, lest you harm a people out of ignorance and become, over what you have done, regretful". " يا أيها الذين آمنوا إن جاءكم فاسق بنبأ فتبينوا أن تصيبوا قومًا بجهالة فتصبحوا على ما فعلتم نادمين". (49:6). Then, the Prophet (PBUH) ordered Al Harith ibn

Abbad ibn Bishr to accompany them in their return in order to collect Zakah.

In another narration, it was reported from Al Harith Derar Al Khuzaie that the Prophet (PBUH) called him to embrace Islam and accept to pay Zakah. So, he did and told the Prophet that he would turn back to his tribe to call them to accept Islam and pay Zakah. And he would collect Zakah from the ones who responded to him. Then, this Zakah would be sent to the Prophet through a messenger he appointed in a due time. The messenger did not come to Al Harith, so, he thought that God and His Prophet became angry with him. Therefore, he decided to go to the Prophet with his tribe. The Prophet (PBUH) sent Al Waleed ibn Uqbah to take the Zakah collected by Al Harith. But Al Waleed did not continue the way to Al Harith because of his fear. So, he returned and told the Prophet: "Al Harith refused to give me the Zakah and was about to kill me". Consequently, the Prophet sent an expedition to Al Harith, who met them on the way and was told about the claim of Al Waleed. When Al Harith reached the Prophet (PBUH), the latter blamed him as a result of the claim. But he swore by God that it was a false claim and he came out of fear anger of the Prophet. Thereupon, the above mentioned verse has been revealed.

The Expedition of Qutba ibn Amer ibn Hadida to Banu Khathaam in Safar

Kaab ibn Malik narrated: The Prophet (PBUH) despatched Qutba ibn Amer ibn Hadida at the head of twenty men to raid against a tribe of Khathaam towards Tabala. The two parties fought each other so severely till Qutba and his companions advocated.

Ibn Saad said that Abu Maashar reported that Qutba ibn Amer fought so tenaciously in the expedition of Badr. Qutba died during the succession of Uthman ibn Affaan (May God be pleased with him), leaving no descendants.

The Expedition of Al Dahhak ibn Sufyan to Banu Kilab in Rabi I

The Prophet (PBUH) despatched Al Dahhak ibn Sufyan at the head of an army against Al Qurata to call them to embrace Islam. They refused, so, they were fought and defeated by the Muslims.

The Expedition of Alqamah ibn Mujazziz Al Mudlaji against Abyssinia in Rabi Al Akhir (the fourth month of the Islamic calendar)

When the Prophet (PBUH) knew that the people of Juddah had gone to the people of Abyssinia, he sent Alqamah Ibn Mujazziz at the head of three hundred persons to the people of Abyssinia. They ran away from him. Some of the companions of Alqamah, among them was Abdullah ibn Hudhafah, hastened to go to their families. So, he was appointed as the leader of those who wanted to go. They halted on the way and enkindled fire to warm themselves. He told them to jump into this fire. When they were about to jump, one of them said to them: Not to hasten till we return to the Prophet (PBUH) and ask him about this. If he orders us to jump into fire, then we will do so. When they returned to the Prophet (PBUH) and told him about what had happened. He replied to them: "If you had entered it, you would have remained there forever. Obedience is obligatory only in what is good".

The Expedition of Ali ibn Abu Talib (May God be pleased with him) to destroy the idol of Al Fuls

The Prophet (PBUH) sent Ali ibn Abu Talib at the head of 150 men of the Ansar in Rabi Al Akhir to demolish the idol of Al Fuls, worshipped by Banu Tayy. So, they destroyed the idol and took two swords which were inside its safe. They captured a lot of sheep and people, among whom was the sister of Adi ibn Hatim – the chief of the tribe of Tayy – who escaped to Syria. His sister was lodged in an enclosure near the door of mosque. When the Prophet (PBUH) passed by her, she told him that her father died and her brother disappeared and she begged him to set her free. The Prophet asked her who was her brother and she informed him that it was Adi ibn Hatim. The Prophet replied: "He is the one who fled from God and His Prophet". The next day she reiterated the same thing to the Prophet (PBUH) and he provided her with clothes, money and a horse to go. When she reached Adi, she blamed him for leaving her behind. He asked her about the Prophet and she replied that she thought he should join the Prophet. Thereupon, Adi came to the Prophet who honored him at his home. Then, Adi embraced Islam.

The Expedition of Ukasha ibn Mihsan to Al Jinab

Al Jinab was the land inhabited by Udhrah and Baliy. This expedition was in Rabi Al Akhir.

The Expedition of Tabuk in Ragab (the seventh month in the Islamic calendar)

The Prophet (PBUH) was informed that the Romans had gathered great troops by the leadership of Heracles and directed to Al Balqaa. So, the Prophet (PBUH) sent to people in Mecca and Arabian tribes in order to fight. And this was in a very hot weather. Some people came to the Prophet to let them participate in the expedition. There were different sayings about their names and number. Abu Saleh reported from ibn Abbas that they were six.

On the other hand, Mujahid said that the verse that has been revealed about them in the Holy Qur'an: "Nor [is there blame] upon those who, when they came to you that you might give them mounts, you said, "I can find nothing for you to ride upon." They turned back while their eyes overflowed with tears out of grief that they could not find something to spend [for the cause of God]". " ولا على الذين إذا ما أتوك لتحملهم قلت لا أجد ما أحملكم عليه تولوا وأعينهم تفيض من الدمع حزنًا ألا يجدوا ما ينفقون" (9:92), is about the descendants of Muqrin and they are seven men. Mohammed ibn Saad mentioned their names: Al Numan ibn Amr ibn Muqrin, Sannan ibn Muqrin, Uqail ibn

Muqrin, Abd Al Rahman ibn Muqrin and Abd Al Rahman ibn Uqail ibn Muqrin.

Some other hypocrite people, their number was eighty odd men, came to the Prophet (PBUH) to allow them not to go for the expedition, although they had no reason for that, and he allowed them what they wanted. And those with excuses among the bedouins came to be permitted to not to go for the expedition but the Prophet (PBUH) did not give them permission. They were eighty two men. The Prophet (PBUH) came to Tabuk at the head of thirty hundred Muslims. Ten hundred ones only among them were on horseback.

This expedition was also called the Hour of Difficulty (Saat Al Usrah), because the Muslims suffered intensive hotness and thirsty and lack of horses to ride. There is a verse in the Holy Qur'an which indicates this name.

Ibn Umar said: On the day of Tabuk, the Prophet (PBUH) passed by Al Hijr region in the land of Thamud with the Muslims. They wanted to drink from the wells of Thamud out of their severe thirsty but the Prophet (PBUH) prohibited them of that. He told them that they could instead drink from the river that the she-camel, the miracle sent by God to the nation of Thamud, was drinking from.

Islamic historical scholars said: The Prophet (PBUH) stayed in Tabuk for twenty days. There was no fighting and Heracles was in the city of Homs.

The Prophet (PBUH) despatched Khalid ibn Al Waleed at the head of four hundred and twenty horse-men to Ukaidir ibn Abd Al Malik – the Christian king of Dumat Al Jandal, the distance from it to Medina took fifteen days. Khalid seized Ukaidir and did not kill him in exchange for conquering Dumat Al Jandal. When Ukaidir was brought to the Prophet (PBUH), the latter spared his life and his brother's life on the condition that they should pay Jizyah.

On the way of the Prophet (PBUH) returning from Tabuk to Medina, some hypocrites mocked at him.

Gabriel informed the Prophet (PBUH) of that concern by the verses God has revealed. When they knew that verses have been revealed about them, they went to the Prophet (PBUH) to make an excuse, saying that they were joking. God says: “And if you ask them, they will surely say, "We were only conversing and playing." Say, "Is it God and His verses and His Messenger that you were mocking?". " وَلَئِن سَأَلْتَهُمْ لَيَقُولُنَّ إِنَّمَا كُنَّا نَخُوضُ وَنَلْعَبُ ۚ قُلْ أَبِاللَّهِ وَآيَاتِهِ وَرَسُولِهِ كُنتُمْ تَسْتَهْزِئُونَ". (9:65). God did not pardon those hypocrites but pardoned one man who repented and did not comply with them. God says to them in the Qur’an: “Make no excuse; you have disbelieved after your belief. If We pardon one faction of you - We will punish another faction because they were criminals”. " لَا تَعْتَذِرُوا قَدْ كَفَرْتُم بَعْدَ إِيمَانِكُمْ ۚ إِن نَّعْفُ عَن طَائِفَةٍ مِّنكُمْ نُعَذِّبْ طَائِفَةً بِأَنَّهُمْ كَانُوا مُجْرِمِينَ". (9:66). “Faction” here means one intended man.

It was narrated by Anas ibn Malik: We returned from the expedition of Tabuk, and when we approached Medina, the Prophet (PBUH) said: "There are some people in Medina who were with you all the time, you did not travel any portion of the journey nor crossed any valley, but they were with you". They (i.e. the people) said, "O Prophet of God! Even though they were at Medina?" He said, "Yes, because they were stopped by a genuine excuse".

The Prophet (PBUH) returned to Medina in Ramadan. The ones who did not go with him for the expedition of Tabuk came to him. He pardoned them and asked God to forgive them. And he adjourned the matter of Kaab ibn Malik and his two companions till the verses of the Holy Qur'an have been revealed about their repentance. People began to sell their weapons and said: There is no longer jihad. When the Prophet (PBUH) knew that, he prohibited them from that and said: "A section of my community will continue to fight for the right and overcome their opponents till the appearance of the Antichrist (Al Dajjal; the Great Deceiver)".

The story of Kaab ibn Malik and his two companions

It was narrated by Abd Al Rahman ibn Abdullah ibn Kaab ibn Malik that his father heard Kaab saying:

"I did not remain behind from any of the battles the Prophet of God (PBUH) fought in, until the battle of Tabuk, except for Badr. And the Prophet (PBUH) did not scold anyone who remained behind from Badr, because he only went out to look for the caravan of Quraysh. The Quraysh came out to help their caravan, so they met without an appointment. I did not accompany the Prophet (PBUH) in the expedition of Tabuk and it was the last one he launched. The Prophet (PBUH) returned in the morning. And when he came back from an expedition, he used to go to the Mosque first and pray two Rakaahs there, then he would sit to meet with the people. Those who had stayed behind came to him and started giving their excuses, swearing by God. He accepted what they declared and accepted their oaths of allegiance; he prayed for forgiveness for them. Then when I came and greeted him, he smiled as one who is angry, then he said: 'Come here'. So I came and sat in front of him, and he said: 'What kept you behind? Did you not buy a mount?' I said: 'O Prophet of God, if I were to sit before anyone other than you of those who hold high positions in this world, I would find a way to avoid his anger. I am an eloquent man but I swear by God I know that if I were to tell you a lie today to make you pleased with me, God would soon make you angry with me. But if I tell you the truth, it will make you angry with me, but I will still have the hope that God may forgive me. I have never been in a better position, physically or financially, than the time when I stayed behind and did not join you'. The Prophet (PBUH) said: 'This man has spoken the truth. Go away until God decides concerning you'. So I got up and went away.

All of the Muslims, even our wives, avoided us for fifty days for our staying behind the Prophet (PBUH) in Tabuk. Then, I was called to go to the Prophet (PBUH) in the Mosque. His face was beaming out of happiness and he said to me: ‘Receive glad tidings of the best day you have seen since your mother bore you!’. So I said: 'O Prophet of God! Is it from God or from you?' He said: 'From God'. Then, the Prophet recited these verses that God has revealed to him: "God has already forgiven the Prophet and the Muhajireen and the Ansar who followed him in the hour of difficulty after the hearts of a party of them had almost inclined [to doubt], and then He forgave them. Indeed, He was to them Kind and Merciful. And [He also forgave] the three who were left behind [and regretted their error] to the point that the earth closed in on them in spite of its vastness and their souls confined them and they were certain that there is no refuge from God except in Him. Then He turned to them so they could repent. Indeed, God is the Accepting of repentance, the Merciful. O you who have believed, fear God and be with those who are true". " لَّقَد تَّابَ اللَّـهُ عَلَى النَّبِيِّ وَالْمُهَاجِرِينَ وَالْأَنصَارِ الَّذِينَ اتَّبَعُوهُ فِي سَاعَةِ الْعُسْرَةِ مِن بَعْدِ مَا كَادَ يَزِيغُ قُلُوبُ فَرِيقٍ مِّنْهُمْ ثُمَّ تَابَ عَلَيْهِمْ ۚ إِنَّهُ بِهِمْ رَءُوفٌ رَّحِيمٌ. وَعَلَى

الثَّلَاثَةِ الَّذِينَ خُلِّفُوا حَتَّىٰ إِذَا ضَاقَتْ عَلَيْهِمُ الْأَرْضُ بِمَا رَحُبَتْ وَضَاقَتْ عَلَيْهِمْ أَنفُسُهُمْ وَظَنُّوا أَن لَّا مَلْجَأَ مِنَ اللَّـهِ إِلَّا إِلَيْهِ ثُمَّ تَابَ عَلَيْهِمْ لِيَتُوبُوا ۚ إِنَّ اللَّـهَ هُوَ التَّوَّابُ الرَّحِيمُ. يَا أَيُّهَا الَّذِينَ آمَنُوا اتَّقُوا اللَّـهَ وَكُونُوا مَعَ الصَّادِقِينَ". (9:117, 9:118, 9:119).

I said: 'O Prophet of God! Because of the acceptance of my repentance I will give up all my wealth as alms for the Sake of God and His Prophet. The Prophet of God (PBUH) said: 'Keep some of your wealth, as it will be better for you'. I said, 'So I will keep my share from Khaybar with me', and added: 'O Prophet of God! God has saved me for telling the truth; so it is a part of my repentance not to tell but the truth as long as I am alive. By God, I do not know anyone of the Muslims whom God has helped for telling the truth more than me. Since I have mentioned that truth to the Prophet of God (PBUH) till today, I have never intended to tell a lie. I hope that God will also save me (from telling lies) the rest of my life.

So after my acceptance of Islam, God did not grant me a greater favor than when I and my two companions told the truth to the Prophet of God (PBUH) and we were not among the liars to be ruined like the others were ruined. God, the Almighty, says about those liars: “They will swear by God to you when you return to them that you would leave them alone. So leave them alone; indeed they are evil; and their refuge is Hell as recompense for what they had been earning. They swear to you so that you might be satisfied with them. But if you should be satisfied with them - indeed, Allah is not satisfied with a defiantly disobedient people". " سَيَحْلِفُونَ بِاللَّـهِ لَكُمْ إِذَا انقَلَبْتُمْ إِلَيْهِمْ لِتُعْرِضُوا عَنْهُمْ ۖ فَأَعْرِضُوا عَنْهُمْ ۖ إِنَّهُمْ رِجْسٌ ۖ وَمَأْوَاهُمْ جَهَنَّمُ جَزَاءً بِمَا كَانُوا يَكْسِبُونَ. يَحْلِفُونَ لَكُمْ لِتَرْضَوْا عَنْهُمْ ۖ فَإِن تَرْضَوْا عَنْهُمْ فَإِنَّ اللَّـهَ لَا يَرْضَىٰ عَنِ الْقَوْمِ الْفَاسِقِينَ". (9:95, 9:96)".

Kaab further added: "The matter of the three of us remained pending for decision apart from the case of those who had made excuses on oath before the Prophet of God (PBUH) and he accepted those, took fresh oaths of allegiance from them and supplicated for their forgiveness. The Prophet (PBUH) kept our matter pending till God decided it. As for God's saying: "And

[He also forgave] the three who were left behind" " وعلى الثلاثة الذين خلفوا". (9:118), the reference here is not to our staying back from the expedition but to his delaying our matter and keeping it pending beyond the matter of those who made their excuses on oath which he accepted".

Among the events occurred in this year was the embracement of Islam of Khuraim ibn Aws

After the return of the Prophet (PBUH) from Tabuk, Khuraim ibn Aws embraced Islam. And Al Abbas praised the Prophet (PBUH) in his famous words.

Among the events occurred in this year after the return of the Prophet (PBUH) from Tabuk was the letter of kings of Himyar to the Prophet, proclaiming their acceptance of Islam

Ibn Isaaq narrated from Abdullah ibn Abu Bakr: A letter was sent to the Prophet (PBUH), upon his return from the expedition to Tabuk, by the kings of Himyar: Al Harith ibn Abd Kolal, Noaim ibn Abd Kolal, Kail Dhu

Roain, Hamadan and Maafir, proclaiming their acceptance of Islam and giving up polytheism. So the Prophet (PBUH) replied to them to be reformers, obey God and His Prophet, perform prayer and give Zakah and charity.

Abu Bakr (May God be pleased with him) performed Hajj (pilgrimage) with the people in Dhul Hijja in this year

The Prophet (PBUH) made Abu Bakr Al Siddiq perform Hajj at the head of three hundred persons and twenty animals to sacrifice. Then, the Prophet (PBUH) ordered Ali ibn Abu Talib (May God be pleased with him) to join Abu Bakr so as to recite Surat Baraa .i.e. Al Tawbah (The Repentance) aloud in public and say: "No pagan shall perform Hajj after this year, and none shall perform the Tawaf around the Kaaba in a naked state". Then, Abu Bakr and Ali turned back to Medina.

The Prophet (PBUH) ordered to demolish Al Dirar Mosque (the Mosque of Dissent)

When Banu Amr ibn Awf built Quba Mosque and sent to the Prophet (PBUH) to pray therein, Banu Ghanam ibn Awf – who were hypocrites among the Ansar – envied them and decided to build a mosque to ask the Prophet (PBUH) to pray therein and to make Abu Amer Al Rahib (a Christian monk) pray therein if he returned from Syria. God, the Mighty and Sublime, has revealed this to the Prophet: "And [there are] those [hypocrites] who took for themselves a mosque for causing harm and disbelief and division among the believers and as a station for whoever had warred against Allah and His Messenger before. And they will surely swear, "We intended only the best." And Allah testifies that indeed they are liars. Do not stand [for prayer] within it". " والذين اتخذوا مسجدًا ضرارًا وكفرًا وتفريقًا بين المؤمنين وإرصادًا لمن حارب الله ورسوله من قبل وليحلفن إن أردنا إلا الحسنى والله يشهد إنهم لكاذبون. لا تقم فيه أبدًا". (9:107, 9:108). Therefore, the Prophet (PBUH) ordered to demolish and burn that mosque.

Stoning the woman from Ghamid

Abdullah ibn Buraida reported on the authority of his father that: A woman from Ghamid came to the Prophet (PBUH) and said: "O Prophet of God, I have committed adultery, so purify me". The Prophet (PBUH) turned her away. On the following day, she said: "O Prophet of God, Why do you turn me away? Perhaps, you turn me away as you turned away Ma'iz. I swear by God that I have become pregnant". He said: "Well, if you insist on it, then go away until you give birth to the baby". When she delivered the baby, she came with him wrapped in a rag and said: "Here is the baby whom I have given birth to". He said: "Go away and suckle him until you wean him". When she had weaned him, she came to the Prophet with the child who was holding a piece of bread in his hand, saying: "O Prophet of God, here is he as I have weaned him and he eats food". The Prophet entrusted the child to one of the Muslims, then he pronounced punishment. She was put in a ditch up to her chest and he commanded people to stone her. Khalid ibn Al Waleed came forward with a stone which he flung at her head and there blood spurted on the face of Khalid, so he abused her. The Prophet (PBUH) heard Khalid cursing her. Thereupon, the Prophet said: "O Khalid, be gentle. By Him in Whose Hand is my life, she has made such a repentance that even if a wrongful tax-collector were to repent, he would have been forgiven". Then giving command regarding her, he prayed over her and she was buried.

The Prophet (PBUH) separated Uwaimir ibn Al Harith Al Ajlani from his wife

This occurred in the Prophet's Mosque, because that man had accused his wife of committing adultery with Sharik ibn Sahma.

Tale of the nobles who died in this year

Al Najashi (named Armah):

He was the one to whom the Muslims migrated. He embraced Islam and did righteous deeds and supported the Muslims. He married Umm Habiba to the Prophet

(PBUH). He died in Ragab of this year. It was narrated from Abu Hurairah that the Prophet (PBUH) announced the death of Al Najashi to the people. Then, he made them align in rows in a place of prayer and said the Takbir – .i.e. God is Greater – four times (performing the Funeral prayer) for him.

Umm Kulthum, the daughter of the Prophet (PBUH)

She married Utba ibn Abu Lahab before the Prophethood. But when God has revealed the verse "May the hands of Abu Lahab be ruined, and ruined is he". "تبت يدا أبي لهب وتب" (111:1), Abu Lahab ordered his son, Utba, to divorce her otherwise he would dissociate himself from him. So, he divorced her before the consummation of marriage. She stayed with the Prophet in Mecca and migrated. In the third year AH, she married Uthman ibn Affan, her brother in law, after the death of her sister Ruqayya. She died in Shaaban. It was narrated from Anas ibn Malik: I saw the Prophet (PBUH) sitting near the grave of her (Umm Kulthum) and his eyes were full of tears. He said, "Is there anyone amongst you who did not have sexual relations with his wife last night?" Abu Talha replied in the affirmative. So, the Prophet told him to get down in her grave.

Suhail ibn Baidaa

He experienced all of the expeditions, including Badr and Uhud, with the Prophet (PBUH). He died at the age of 40 after the return of the Prophet (PBUH) from the expedition to Tabuk. And the Prophet (PBUH) performed the Funeral prayer for him. The aged ones among the companions of the Prophet (PBUH) were Abu Bakr and Suhail ibn Baidaa.

Abdullah ibn Abd Nahm ibn Afif

He was a poor orphan. So, he was put in the care of his uncle till he became rich. He longed for embracing Islam when the Prophet (PBUH) came to Medina. But he knew that his uncle rejected Islam. Years later, he asked his uncle to allow him to embrace Islam. But his uncle threatened him that he would take everything he had given him even the clothes he wore if he embraced Islam. However, Abdullah decided to embrace Islam and forsake idol worship. So, his uncle carried out his threat. Then, he went to Medina and met the Prophet (PBUH) in the Mosque. The Prophet (PBUH) taught him the Holy Qur'an. So, he kept on reading it aloud. Then, he desired for martyrdom in the expedition of Tabuk. He died while they were staying in Tabuk.

Abdullah ibn Ubayy ibn Malik ibn Al Harith ibn Ubaid – ibn Salul

He was the noblest of the tribe of Al Khazraj before they embraced Islam. When the Prophet (PBUH) came to Medina and the people honored him, he envied the Prophet and became a hypocrite. He died after the return of the Prophet from the expedition to Tabuk.

Muaawiah ibn Muaawiah Al Laithy, named Al Muzani

He died in Medina while the Prophet (PBUH) was in the expedition to Tabuk.

.

CHAPTER 8

The Tenth Year After Hijrah (AH)

Among the events that took place in this year:

The Prophet (PBUH) sent Khalid ibn Al Waleed to Banu Al Harith ibn Kaab

It was narrated from Abdullah ibn Abu Bakr that the Prophet (PBUH) sent Khalid ibn Al Waleed in the tenth year AH to Banu Al Harith ibn Kaab in Najran, so as to call them to embrace Islam and teach them the Qur'an and Sunnah. So, they accepted Islam and a delegation among them came with Khalid to the Prophet (PBUH), saying: "We witness that you are the Prophet of God and there is no deity but God". When their delegation returned Najran, the Prophet (PBUH) sent to them Amr ibn Al Harith Al Ansary to teach them Fiqh, Sunnah and Islamic Laws and collect charity.

The coming of the delegation of Salaman to the Prophet (PBUH) in Shawwal

They were seven persons who came to pledge to the Prophet (PBUH) that they would embrace Islam.

The coming of the delegation of Muharib to the Prophet (PBUH) in Farewell Pilgrimage (Hajjat Al Wadaa)

It was narrated from Abu Wajza Al Saadi that: The delegation of Muharib were ten persons who came to the Prophet (PBUH) to embrace Islam. Among them was a man who said to the Prophet (PBUH): "Praise be to God Who lets me alive till I believe in you". The Prophet (PBUH) replied to him: "These hearts are in the hand of God". The Prophet (PBUH) honored them like any other delegation. Then, they went out.

The coming of the delegation of Al Azd to the Prophet (PBUH)

Surd ibn Abdullah Al Azdi was at the head of them. After he embraced Islam, the Prophet made him the leader of the Muslims in his people.

The coming of the delegations of Ghassan and Aamela to the Prophet (PBUH)

Both of them happened in Ramadan.

The coming of the delegation of Zubaid to the Prophet (PBUH)

It was narrated from Abdullah ibn Abu Bakr that Amr ibn Maadi Karb headed a delegation of Banu Zubaid and came to the Prophet (PBUH) proclaiming that they have embraced Islam. When the Prophet (PBUH) died, Amr reverted from Islam then turned back to it.

The coming of the delegation of Abd Al Qais to the Prophet (PBUH)

Ibn Isaaq said: A delegation of Abd Al Qais, led by Al Garoud ibn Amr who was a Christian, came to the Prophet (PBUH) and embraced Islam.

The coming of the delegation of Kinda to the Prophet (PBUH)

They were under the leadership of Al Ashaath ibn Qais. They came to embrace Islam.

The coming of the delegation of Banu Hanifa, including Musailamah the liar, to the Prophet (PBUH)

Musailamah ibn Habib Al Hanafy was among this delegation. They embraced Islam but when they arrived at Yamama, Musailamah, the enemy of God, reverted from Islam and claimed he was a prophet.

The coming of the delegation of Bajila to the Prophet (PBUH)

They were one hundred and fifty men, led by Jarir ibn Abdullah Al Bajaly. They embraced Islam. Then, the Prophet (PBUH) sent Jarir to demolish the idol of Dhul Khalasa.

• •

The End

The End of Part 3

www.ingramcontent.com/pod-product-compliance
Ingram Content Group UK Ltd.
Pitfield, Milton Keynes, MK11 3LW, UK
UKHW021036270726
13967UKWH00013B/2814